Black Pandering

Why Racism May Never End

Charles G. Ankrom

authorHOUSE

AuthorHouse™
1663 Liberty Drive
Bloomington, IN 47403
www.authorhouse.com
Phone: 1 (800) 839-8640

© 2015 Charles G. Ankrom. All rights reserved.

No part of this book may be reproduced, stored in a retrieval system, or transmitted by any means without the written permission of the author.

Published by AuthorHouse   07/13/2015

ISBN: 978-1-5049-2120-6 (sc)
ISBN: 978-1-5049-2121-3 (e)

Library of Congress Control Number: 2015910760

Print information available on the last page.

Any people depicted in stock imagery provided by Thinkstock are models, and such images are being used for illustrative purposes only.
Certain stock imagery © Thinkstock.

This book is printed on acid-free paper.

Because of the dynamic nature of the Internet, any web addresses or links contained in this book may have changed since publication and may no longer be valid. The views expressed in this work are solely those of the author and do not necessarily reflect the views of the publisher, and the publisher hereby disclaims any responsibility for them.

Foreword

The pandering to blacks and their cries of racism by society and the media has gotten worse and worse over time.

It seems you cannot turn on the television or listen to any news broadcasts which do not include yet another report about a situation where blacks are claiming discrimination and racism.

In recent years, all that seemed to be on the news were the stories of the deaths of Trayvon Martin, Michael Brown, and Eric Garner, at the hands of white cops, or neighborhood watchmen. And virtually all of that news was slanted along the lines of racial injustices having been committed.

The race card was not only played and played heavily, but society, fueled by the media, allowed it. In fact, they not only allowed it, they ate it up, as they pandered excessively to blacks.

And even though juries, and grand juries, cleared the white cops or neighborhood watchmen of any wrongdoing in these cases, these cries of racism didn't abate, but got worse.

We continue to hear these cries of racism over and over again, and it seems to be true for every little situation. It has become eerily similar to the story of 'the little boy who cried wolf.'

The degree of this pandering to blacks has reached epic proportions, perhaps according to a notion I propose in these pages of a politically-correct mindset of reverse discrimination. That is, that our society, driven by the media, has fallen hook, line and sinker for all these cries of discrimination and racism to the point that it is now assumed that in any of these situations it will be accepted, presumed, if you will, that whites have discriminated against blacks, and even to the point that it results in reverse discrimination.

Charles G. Ankrom

I cover many areas of life today where this storyline is played out over and over and over again. Be it politics, the criminal justice system, education, sports, or even entertainment, discrimination by whites against blacks is simply presumed and accepted by society and the media.

I further submit herein the notion that racism itself will never end if this excessive black pandering and politically-correct mindset of reverse discrimination continues.

The silent white majority is tired of having this racism crammed down their throats, and especially in situations where facts turn out to prove that these cries are unjustified. Most of these individuals, including myself, are truly in favor of a racially equal world, but due to the excess of the pandering to blacks have no real desire to exert the effort needing to achieving that world.

Tell me about those instances where true discrimination occurs (where the wolf is actually present) and I will be the first to address it. (I, for one, do feel that charges should have been filed in the Eric Garner case, and even the more recent Freddie Gray case)

But to gripe and complain (cry wolf) about every little thing?

The Oscars are too white?

A rodeo clown wearing an Obama mask at a state fair is racist?

Give me a break!

And the degree to which the media of today panders to blacks for every little claim of discrimination and racism has become, quite honestly, sickening.

And last but not least this book presents my notion that a 'thug mentality' exists among blacks which, along with the pandering to blacks and the politically-correct mindset of reverse discrimination poses a barrier to ever ending racism.

An insurmountable barrier? Only time will tell.

I ask that you please not consider me or this book racist. For I and it are clearly not. I am merely presenting one view for you to consider, and attempting to provide sufficient facts for my ideas to have merit.

Please allow yourself to read the words herein with an open mind, and agree or disagree.

But above all, try to consider if the words and my notions herein could be true.

Perhaps this book can be the start of the true dialogue between the races that is needed for racism to end!

Prologue

Imagine a movie trailer as it comes across your television screen. "Now playing at a theater near you. 'Black Men Can't Read.' Starring Woody Harrelson and Wesley Snipes. (or some other popular Hollywood acting duo consisting of one white actor and one black one) Rated R for language and urban humor."

"Watch and enjoy the antics as our duo travel across the country as a two-man college history bowl team competing against other college history bowl teams. Except the other teams are always comprised of white people!"

"Things get dicey as the real story line unfolds of how our two guys are in it solely to make money by betting on the matches, by hustling the other all-white teams to assume that because one of our players is….. GULP…. BLACK, our team will most surely be a pushover, a shoe-in, a sure thing!"

In this imagined movie, Harrelson's character, and the other team's members all wear suits and ties. The women wear dresses.

Our black Snipes character wears urban wear (whatever your definition of that might be). Picture a tank top which accentuates heavy tattoos up and down both arms. Shiny jewelry and bling and even a gold tooth or two.

A flat-billed ball cap sits slightly ajar on his head hiding only some of his dread locks and corn rows and his baggy pants hang so low you can see the plaid boxers sticking out the back.

That should do it.

He needs to appear the part of a black, urban, probably uneducated, thug, helping the other white history bowlers to buy in to the perception that he probably can't be very smart.

Remember Harrelson's character from "White Men Can't Jump?" He was about the most non-athletic, clumsily-dressed and awkward-acting white guy imaginable. Dopey hat, clothes that looked nerdy even.

He had to sell the other black basketball players the perception that he probably wasn't very good at the game, especially the way it was played on the street.

You get the picture.

The other all-white history bowlers assume there's no way Snipes can be good at history, "I mean. He's BLACK!"

Even one white member of a team from a college in the South had the audacity to lean over to his also-Southern also-white teammate and whisper, "Can you believe they brought a (pause) N*****? (as his voice is drowned out by laughter from the other teams)

And these all-white teams, knowing the national statistics of black people dropping out of and not finishing high school (I mean they should know, they're history bowlers!) much less ever attending or graduating from college, are duped into a false sense of security in going up against Harrelson and Snipes.

To build up the ruse, our two connivers let the preliminary matches go much along the lines that the all-white teams have been set up to assume. Harrelson and Snipes get their asses kicked.

Why, Snipe's character doesn't even know the capital of New York! He says New York City with all the bravado that an urban black thug can muster. (Everyone knows it's Albany!)

Taking advantage of this assumption of the all-white teams, our guys then propose to bet on the following matches. And from that point on they answer all the questions and consistently win because the hustle in our movie is that it just so happens that Snipes is a super genius at history, extremely intelligent, and not the stereotypical black person that he was assumed, and pretending to be.

Sounds funny huh?

In fact, it's very similar to "White Men Can't Jump," except for, and only except for the fact that the races are reversed.

The potential for a hilarious comedy, right?

No?

Or?

Racist?

Let me ask you a question. What's the first thing you thought of when you began reading this chapter about my proposed movie? The first thing? Be honest. Did you wonder in your mind how someone in their right mind could ever think about making a movie called "Black Men Can't Read"?

Especially in the society in which we live?

And then as you continued to read the description of my imaginary movie, "Black Men Can't Read" did you wonder how someone could so blatantly disparage blacks, and use words and descriptions which so obviously appear to humiliate this minority group of people?

Or at least did you wonder for a minute how anyone could ever say, or write, such things in public?

If you had such thoughts and the word 'racist' came to your mind even ever so slightly, and I dare suggest that it did, then the very point of this book might just have already been made.

Because if you had such thoughts about my imaginary movie, but laughed yourself silly in the 1990's when Woody Harrelson and Wesley Snipes brought the house down with fun and laughter in their actual 1992 box-office hit "White Men Can't Jump" then yes, my friend, the purpose and point of this book has for sure already been made.

For I am guessing you did NOT entertain thoughts of 'that's racist' when, "White Men Can't Jump" came out.

But like millions of others who flooded the box office to the tune of some $90 million worldwide (one of the top grossing films of 1992) you probably never even thought that "White Men Can't Jump" was racist, should not be allowed, or should be criticized because of its obvious and blatant racism.

I for one, don't remember anyone ever suggesting that "White Men Can't Jump" was racist.

To be honest and fair, the makers of the movie stayed away from dialogue and other things that might cause people to cry racism about the actual contents of the movie, but the innuendos were definitely there, and the very premise of the movie-- that white men were assumed to be inferior to blacks in playing basketball and a couple of hustlers would use that to make a living by betting on the games, was unequivocally as racist as racist can be., and right there on marquees all across America!

But nothing about racism was said.

Nothing.

Everyone simply laughed.

Which brings me to the purpose and point of this book--to intellectually acknowledge, discuss and hopefully prove my proposition that there exists in our society something which I shall call a politically-correct mindset of reverse discrimination.

Black Pandering

Black pandering, if you will. That blacks in our society are pandered to every time they scream racism. In all areas of life--politics, sports, entertainment, education, the criminal justice system. You name it.

The national media, or most of it, are just as responsible as the blacks who scream racism, as the national spotlight is so easily shone on all incidents where blacks claim to have been discriminated against by whites. "White cop shoots black teen" "Police are guilty of racial profiling" are just some of the refrains we constantly seem to hear.

But we never, NEVER, hear the other side of the story, where the roles are reversed. And this pandering to blacks is so blatant and permitted by society and the media, that it has become an ingrained, politically-correct mindset.

This mindset is a universally accepted assumption, a presumption, a given if you will, that blacks are always discriminated against by whites in our society, and that society must do something, everything it can, to remedy this discrimination.

Now, if the discussion simply ended here, with doing away with discrimination against blacks, there would be no problem. There would be no need for this book. Doing away with all discrimination should be the goal of society.

But the problem which this book discusses, is that the application of, or the living out of this politically-correct mindset in society has been taken to an extreme from which we may never return.

For this massive, almost conditioned, effort by society to appease this presumed discrimination by whites against blacks has become so 'politically-correct' as that term has come to be used in society, that the backlash has produced results of actual, verifiable 'politically-correct,' or socially accepted, discrimination by blacks against whites, or reverse discrimination.

The first example of this I have already given you.

We all know there's no way in hell society would ever allow a movie to exist called "Black Men Can't Read" without it being racist, even though they tripped all over themselves in receiving, praising, and accepting the movie, "White Men Can't Jump."

But I also have a second proposition--that these extreme inequalities and inequities being lived out each and every day in our society may have reached a point, accompanied by what I call the existence of a 'thug mentality' or 'thug culture,' where they pose a major, if not insurmountable barrier to ever obtaining true equality between blacks and whites.

Yep.

Racism may never end, or at least as long as this mindset exists, and this excessive pandering to blacks continues.

This book contains examples, proof if you will, of this politically-correct mindset of reverse discrimination in our society over the past decade or so.

These examples are from all parts of life--the world of sports, politics, crime, entertainment, etc.

As you follow the timelines of some of these examples, you can see how this mindset has grown stronger and stronger with the passage of time, how the pandering has gotten worse and worse.

We have all witnessed these examples being played out in our society (and I lay a great deal of blame on the role our national media has played) but these examples have never, until this book perhaps, been brought together, recognized and discussed intelligently, nor posed to the reader to seriously consider whether the ideas herein could be true.

I challenge you to read and see if these examples do not, in fact, support my proposition of the existence of a politically-correct mindset of reverse discrimination, or black pandering.

Agree with me, disagree with me, but above all open up your mind as you read and seriously consider if this proposition is true.

Because if it is true, then we must, as a society, seriously consider the second part of my proposition about whether there can ever be true equality between blacks and whites until this politically-correct mindset of reverse discrimination is done away with and the pandering ceases.

Will there ever be a time when we can all live in a world where people are not black, or white, (or African American, Hispanic, or Asian for that matter), but just 'people'?

Imagine a world where equal is finally equal!

Chapter 1: Why This Book?

To be honest, I had long planned to write this book. I began to get the idea for it way back when the movie "White Men Can't Jump" first came out in 1992.

I wondered then why no one saw that movie as racist. Instead, people from all ethnic groups plopped down their money to see it, and laughed their heads off.

To think, here was a movie poking fun at a perceived inadequacy of white people to black (i.e. the inability to jump, or more precisely, to play basketball).

Now, it was not openly racist in the way it was made or in the dialogue, and I give the movie makers credit for that.

But the premise of the movie was clearly there, in the title of the movie, written out on marquees all across America-- "White Men Can't Jump," and in the innuendoes and storyline.

But not one thing was said about racism. Nothing.

I thought to myself then about my imagined movie, "Black Men Can't Read" and wondered what society would say if I had made just such a movie.

I dare say I would have been crucified for such blatant racism. Strung up, perhaps. Oops, I probably shouldn't use that phrase because that is racist too, at least when used by a white person. Starting to see the picture?

I began to perceive what was obvious to me, but apparently not to anyone else—the existence of a politically-correct mindset of reverse discrimination in our society.

How could discrimination simply be assumed in our society when it was whites discriminating against blacks, but not when it flowed the other direction?

Be that as it may, I also paid my money to watch the movie, laughed some myself and filed my feelings away, thinking that perhaps it was just one example, and maybe I was being too critical in drawing what to me was the obvious conclusion.

I did nothing, I guess the lazy part of me was thinking that we were becoming a more equal society and that things would continue to get better as far as equality and fairness was concerned.

I was wrong.

Through the years, I continued to notice other incidents and occurrences which further pointed out this politically-correct mindset of reverse discrimination, and the thought of writing the book continued to grow.

Further, I began to notice how newspapers and television news stories started pandering to blacks every time they cried racism. I watched as these stories were given not just the time of day, but the biggest spotlight of all.

And this pandering to blacks crying racism got worse and worse with the passage of time.

Remember the attention paid to the death of Trayvon Martin, and the circus that was the trial of George Zimmerman? And how about the entire fall of 2014 and how the media world was obsessed with the death of Michael Brown in Ferguson, and then Eric Garner in New York? Cover the cries of racism, at all cost.

Yet we never heard about the stories where the roles were reversed, did we? Many of these incidents are covered in detail in the chapters that follow.

I think back to the time I went to watch the Harlem Globetrotters in Springfield, Missouri in the mid 1990's. As I watched in a gym that was filled with an audience that was approximately 95% white, I suddenly realized that a great deal of their humor and jokes were quite simply racist.

Meadowlark Lemon at one point was in the crowd talking to a spectator and looked as if he had lost track of where she was sitting and remarked, "well, you people do all look alike."

The crowd roared.

It was "White Men Can't Jump" all over again.

The other team, which was at least 90 percent white, and even the white referees were maligned with jokes that were blatantly racist.

Were people mad? Were they leaving the gym because of the racism?

No.

They were laughing.

And everyone seemed to leave with a smile on their face, because black people making fun of white people was politically-correct in our society.

I thought of my history bowl movie scenario once more, about all the white members on the other teams making fun of how stupid the black guy on our team obviously had to be. I mean, "Black Men Can't Read," right?

I wondered again how that would go over as a movie in society, much less if it happened for real.

It wouldn't.

There was a clear double standard-- a politically-correct mindset of reverse discrimination.

I began to notice other things that supported my proposition as well, and watched as the presumption grew so much more ingrained with the passage of time.

The pandering continued, and grew!

Black comedians could use the N-word and make all the jokes about white people they wanted to, without ramifications. White comedians, and all other whites for that matter, could not.

Famous white celebrities and entertainers, from Fuzzy Zoeller in golf, to Don Imus on the talk show circuit, either lost, or severely damaged their careers for making racial comments against blacks. Many of these instances are covered in later chapters of this book.

Black civil rights activists such as Jesse Jackson and Al Sharpton flocked to the scenes of any incident where whites were allegedly discriminating against blacks, or where whites made racial comments against blacks.

They demanded justice in the name of equality. And society, and the media, graciously accepted their presence as well as their ramblings.

I didn't see the same men, or anyone else for that matter go to the incidents where it was alleged that blacks had mistreated, or discriminated against, or said racial comments against whites.

Why not?

Perhaps you, too, are beginning to see the point of this book.

On and on, the examples came to life.

We have a Congressional Black Caucus in Washington, D.C. Is there a Congressional White one?

We have a Black History Month, but I don't recall there being a white one of those either!

Affirmative Action where thousands of white lost jobs, or positions in educational enrollments, to blacks.

Over and over, events played out this recurring theme of a politically-correct mindset of reverse discrimination and an excessive pandering of blacks.

One chapter herein covers the incident of the Jena Six in Louisiana and the arrival in criminal law of something called 'hate crimes' which society seems to use predominantly for crimes of whites against blacks and not the reverse.

My chapter and discussion on the Jena six will clearly illustrate how the use of 'hate crimes' analysis in that particular incident almost single-handedly proves my propositions.

And then one day, it happened. Something which finally triggered me to begin to pen these thoughts, facts, and ideas.

But I didn't want to just gripe and complain.

Everybody does that.

Nor did I want to come across as some sort of white supremacist or racist, for either of those I am truly not.

I believe in equality for all races of people.

I had a sincere hope to present my views in an intellectual way that not only proved the existence of a politically-correct mindset of reverse discrimination, but backed it up with examples and instances in a way that people could actually recognize the existence of it themselves.

And in doing so, perhaps they could be motivated in a positive way to do something about it and bring about an end to racism.

The trigger was an article which appeared on the front page, no less, of the Springfield, Missouri News-Leader on January 17, 2011. This is the same

Springfield where I had previously watched the Harlem Globetrotter game earlier.

Now Springfield has the distinction of being the second least diverse city in America (behind Portland, Oregon) for a town its size. The percentage of all minorities who live there is extremely small.

The article was about the local Springfield chapter of the NAACP organizing a visit for black high school students from Springfield to visit some 'historically black colleges' (also discussed in chapters herein) in Missouri so they could, and I quote the local NAACP head, "show them young people who look like them" who were successfully achieving at a college level.

Did the NAACP leader actually say that?

Clearly, that had to be one of the most blatantly racist things anyone could ever say.

Period.

And right there, no less, than on the front page of Springfield's daily newspaper.

But the way the story was written made it appear to be such a wonderful thing that these black high school students were going to go to a 'historically black college' (know of any 'historically white colleges' that still exist as such, by the way?) so they could see other students who "look like them" and therefore want to achieve the same.

You have got to be kidding me, I thought.

I watched the same newspaper for days to see if anyone picked up on the racist aspect of the story the way I did.

Not one letter to the editor.

None.

I got to wondering what might happen if I had organized a trip for inner-city white high school students from say, Kansas City, Missouri, which has a large black population, to go to some almost all white rural Missouri school to see other white students achieving, other students who "look like them" being successful in school.

You and I both know, that I would never have heard the end of that as being absolutely and totally racist. .

Clearly there existed in our society a politically-correct mindset of reverse discrimination, and an excess of pandering to blacks. I realized then and there that something finally needed to be said.

And thus began "Black Pandering: Why Racism May Never End." or a book centered around an opening idea of a proposed move called "Black Men Can't Read."

Totally fictitious, of course. For there never was, is, or will be, such a movie.

And that's the point. Society would never allow such a racist movie to be made. Yet "White Men Can't Jump" was never even slightly considered racist.

I continued to gather ideas, and society didn't let me down!

More and more white celebrities fell by the wayside for uttering that dreaded N word.

Heck, society even had to create the euphemism—N word, to refer to the N word. You couldn't even use the word when talking about the word!

Or at least whites couldn't!

But wait, blacks could use the N word at will. Whites were told it was a word of 'endearment' among blacks. Hogwash!

And the word currently proliferates the rap music of today.

Then came the death of Trayvon Martin. The media exploded in an attempt to make Trayvon's death a racial thing. CNN even had to create, or at least use the most, the term, "white Hispanic" to describe George Zimmerman, Trayvon's killer, to even make the story a racial one, because Zimmerman was not actually white, but Hispanic.

And alas, Zimmerman was found not guilty. And society, due to the politically-correct mindset of reverse discrimination had a racial injustice on its hands, where once again the whites had discriminated against the blacks.

Protests were rampant, with protestors proclaiming the beginning of a new civil rights movement. "Justice for Trayvon" they shouted. But some of the jurors from the trial threw a little kink in that plan by proclaiming that race played no role whatsoever in their decision.

I am sure you remember all the attention paid to the death of Trayvon Martin, and the circus that was the trial of George Zimmerman?

And how about the entire fall of 2014 and how the media world was obsessed with the death of Michael Brown in Ferguson, and then Eric Garner in New York? Cover the cries of racism, at all cost.

Yet we never heard about the stories where the roles were reversed, did we? Many of these incidents are covered in detail in the chapters that follow.

There were a few years of quiet after that, then boom—Ferguson, and the death of the unarmed black teenager Michael Brown by white cop Darren Wilson.

The entire fall of 2014 the media world was obsessed with the death of Michael Brown in Ferguson. Cover the cries of racism, at all cost.

Story after story after story. Pandering to a degree previously not seen.

All we heard about was Ferguson and Michael Brown.

Again discrimination of whites against blacks was alleged and allowed by society and the media to be presumed, especially after the grand jury of St Louis County refused to indict.

Protests broke out. Violence erupted. Blacks were shouting, "No justice, No peace," or "Hands up don't shoot." The spotlight of the media was clearly Ferguson and just as clearly the news was slanted toward the black point of view.

Whites seemed to remember, "Burn this Bitch Down," or the words of Brown's step father Louis Head just before the violence, (and fires) broke out.

And maybe that was what whites wanted to hear based on the excessive pandering of blacks that seemed to be the special of the day.

Shortly after that came another boom. The death of Eric Garner in Staten Island, New York City. Again a failure to indict. Riots and protests broke out anew.

Now it was, "Black lives matter" and a full blown revival of racism in America. The media ate it up and crammed it down the throats of all Americans, further calling for investigations from the administration of America's first black president.

The Department of Justice obliged, as to the Garner and Brown killings, even though they failed to announce separate investigations in the deaths of several whites at the hands of blacks. (again, explained in later chapters herein)

Double standards were everywhere.

The politically-correct mindset of reverse discrimination, rather than having subsided, was worse than ever, or so it seemed.

And the pandering reached epic proportions, even up to today through the recent death of Freddie Gray in Baltimore.

Pandering to blacks?

You tell me.

You remember how the death of Freddie Gray was clearly made a racial issue?

Try this on for size.

Three of the six cops charged in Freddie Gray's death are BLACK, the police chief of Baltimore is BLACK, the mayor of Baltimore is BLACK, and the district attorney of Baltimore is BLACK.

Yet somehow it was all made into a racial injustice issue and a "Black Lives Matter" revival by blacks and the media.

The book had to be finished.

So here it is!

"Black Pandering: Why Racism May Never End."

Chapter 2: "The Animal"

In entertaining my thoughts over the years of writing this book, and wondering exactly how I might get my ideas across in words, I was never so utterly shocked as when I entered a movie theater in 2001 and watched what appeared to be just another routine light-hearted comedy.

The move was called 'The Animal" and starred popular comedian Rob Schneider. You may remember him from Saturday Night Live.

The movie was funny, but for me at least, turned out to be far from routine, at least to my way of thinking.

Because as I walked out of the theater that night I realized that never had the very point and proposition of my book been so vividly presented.

There it was as plain as day!

It was in the form of a comedy, but we all know that sometimes the truest truths come across best that way.

You truly need to rent and watch that movie if the ideas contained in this book interest you at all, and see for yourself.

The movie 'The Animal" which grossed some $84 million, was about Schneider's character being critically injured but unknown to him, put back together by a mad scientist using animal parts.

Yes, animal parts.

As a result, Schneider's character began to exhibit strange, but permanent, and uncontrollable changes in his behavior.

Essentially, he began to act like an animal.

Now, in what appeared to be a side story to the overall storyline was Schneider's black male friend who was always claiming the existence of reverse discrimination as to him because he was black.

No matter how hard he tried, it seemed he could never get anyone white to hold him responsible for anything, even for things he had actually done. Several times during the movie he was seen complaining about this reverse discrimination.

And it wouldn't be until the very end of the movie that we learned how the black friend's character and his issues were going to be woven into a resolution of the entire movie.

As the movie progressed, Schneider first noticed some minor, but weird changes in is behavior. He would jump for frisbees, chase cats and generally exhibit animal-like tendencies.

He developed a super sense of smell, and in one hilarious scene helped sniff out heroin in the rectum of a man at an airport. He was awarded a medal by the police.

These changes in his behavior, however, got stronger and stronger. Further, he could not control them.

He woke up one morning in a strange place and did not even remember his activities from the night before. He heard about some animal attacks that had been committed during the night and he, along with moviegoers alike, assumed the attacks were committed by him.

Eventually, the police began suspecting him due to his suspicious behaviors and actions and began looking for him.

Upon hearing this and being afraid that he was responsible for the attacks Schneider ran off into the woods.

The police, accompanied by an angry mob, in a scene made to look very similar to the old black and white "Frankenstein" movies, followed him into the woods.

Just as the mob was about to confront him, the mad scientist responsible for Schneider's animal characteristics arrived and told him there was another patient, (up to this point a fact unknown to Schneider and to moviegoers) who had also received animal parts and who was out of control and was the one actually responsible for the animal attacks.

But the other animal happened to be Schneider's girlfriend in the movie, who jumped out of the bushes at this point to join him.

The police and the angry mob found them both together and were about to kill them, to lynch them if you will, when Schneider's black male friend, who could never get blamed for anything according to his allegations of reverse discrimination, stepped forward.

He attempted to take the blame for all the of the vicious attacks, even though it was obvious to moviegoers that he was clearly not guilty of anything. He once again claimed that because he was black no one would ever hold him accountable for anything due to reverse discrimination.

Sure enough, once the mob began to listen to this blacks guy's story and believe that he was responsible, they immediately changed their tune.

"Oh no, not a black guy," or so it appeared the mob members were thinking.

You could tell they wanted absolutely no part of violence against a black person. For it would surely be assumed that they were discriminating against the black guy simply because he was black.

Even one mob member, played by Norm Macdonald voiced the feelings of the mob, "I'm never gonna be part of a mob to kill a black guy. I'll tell you that."

One by one the mob dispersed, disheartened.

And thus, the movie ended, with everyone living happily ever after.

Here it was entirely. My proposition. In movie form.

The white mob was recognizing that society would never stand for them punishing a black guy. It would be assumed they were discriminating against him because, and simply because, he was black.

Funny it was, and so vivid in its presentation of the existence of a politically-correct mindset of reverse discrimination.

Again, I urge you to rent and watch the movie and see if you don't agree.

Chapter 3: The National Association for the Advancement of Colored People

The National Association for the Advancement of Colored People, or NAACP, has been around since 1909. Over the years the influence of the NAACP has been tremendous and far-reaching.

Chapters of the NAACP have sprang up in most, if not all the states, and chapters have been set up in many of our larger cities.

And you can't argue with the fact that a lot of good things have been accomplished by the NAACP over the years which have contributed greatly to helping bring about equality between the races.

It's somewhat odd, though, that their website, to the extent I found, refers predominantly to the organization by its abbreviation of NAACP. Only three times, including once in the group's logo is the word 'colored' even found.

The group claims the original name is retained in accordance with tradition. It seems the tradition in society of using the word 'colored', however, has long since passed, it having become politically-incorrect, or even just plain racist, for that word to be used when referring to blacks, at least as far as being used by white people.

The funny part is that the NAACP, and their continued use of the word 'colored' in their very title has grown so strong and accepted in our society that I can never see them changing their name to get rid of the word.

Further it appears that society has accepted the word's usage by the NAACP without even giving it the time of day.

I have begun to notice in recent years that blacks have started to refer to themselves as "people of color" once again, so perhaps the phrase is making a comeback.

The NAACP annually gives out its Image Awards, given in achievement in arts, movies, and entertainment on deserving black Americans. The Image Awards is an awards show much like other awards shows of our day, live and on national media. This year's show was on TV One on February 6.

The NAACP also puts out an annual Spingarn Award, named after Joel Elias Springarn, for outstanding achievement by an African American.

I don't seem to know of any award show for arts and entertainment devoted entirely to the achievements of white people

Do you?

How about it? The Oscars, and Emmys and similar entertainment awards already include black people.

So why the need for, and why does society so willingly accept, even the existence of such Image Awards?

Again, it's the mindset that I have identified herein that permeates our thought culture, and the pandering of blacks that has developed which perpetuates it.

The actual vision of the NAACP, from their website is to "ensure a society in which all individuals have equal rights without discrimination based on race." This sounds like a noble cause for sure. No one can argue with that.

But even though they claim to stand for racial equality for everyone, it seems, in practice, their actions are almost entirely for and on behalf of blacks.

Does this practice not make the group itself racist?

You decide.

I bet the NAACP would stand up and challenge me at this point and try to say that, indeed, they stand up for all races.

Well I would challenge them right back. Show me cases or situations where you have stood up for white people. How many times has that happened? Let me see how the numbers break down, the percentages of cases for each of the races.

And I will add another part to my challenge. Change your name. Call yourselves the National Association for the Advancement of All People.

Guess what? It won't happen.

A recent controversy the NAACP was involved in was surrounding their passage of a resolution condemning "explicit racial behavior" by supporters of the Tea Party movement, implicitly accusing the Tea Party of being racist.

I have to stop here and ask--How in the world is that not the pot calling the kettle black?

How does a group that is so arguably by name, acts, and deeds, as racist as a group could ever be, get by in this world calling another group racist?

But they did seem to get away with it, and I suggest it was because they are a black group calling a white group racist, again something that is readily accepted in society according to my proposition.

And even though the Tea Party condemned the NAACP for "hypocritically engaging in the very conduct they purport to oppose," the bulk of the national media and of society in general seemed to openly accept the organization's condemnations and no one questioned whether they too had been guilty of using racist language in their past, or racial behavior to achieve their goals.

They are the NAACP for gosh sake! They can say and do anything they please. They even went so far as to develop an online 'Tea Party tracker' project to monitor the group, essentially telling the Tea Party--"we're watching you."

Seriously? Yes.

Another part of the problem with the NAACP as I see it, is simply the immense power of the NAACP. The last thing our political leaders want is the NAACP coming down on them. So political candidates from presidential nominees on down cater to and court the NAACP.

Blatant pandering!

I think I even recall President George W. Bush, upon entering the U.S. House of Representative's chamber to make one of his State of the Union speeches, make a special point to stop and shake hands with the leader of the NAACP. I wondered at the time why he needed to do that, and more importantly why was the leader of the NAACP even there? I didn't get an invitation to that one. Did you?

The NAACP issues an Opportunity and Diversity Report Card for the Hotel and Lodging industry which analyzes the largest companies on their representation of African Americans and people of color as a whole with respect to workplace, supplier diversity, and ownership. And once again, it's the publicity they generate and the widespread acceptance of their publicity which is alarming and helps to support the proposition of this book.

The group also grades the members of U.S. Congress's actions with their Legislative Report Card, which has been issued since 1914. It is by definition intended to be useful in efforts to educate NAACP members, and other Americans, on civil rights votes of critical importance to the African American community. In it the Senators and Representatives are assigned grades on their votes, according to the wishes and goals of the NAACP, of course.

Last year for instance 46 percent of Senators and 55 percent of Representatives got an "F" for their efforts in addressing civil rights (you can read that as black, or colored) issues.

And when the NAACP talks, society listens.

We pander to blacks that cry racism, remember?

Were there any white groups who graded congressional efforts on behalf of whites at all, much less any white groups whose grades would have been given the time of day and not merely labeled racist? No.

Local chapters of the group make themselves visible and vocal in communities where criminal law incidents occur. The problem with this isn't so much that they attempt to intervene, or even that it tends to always be for and on behalf of blacks, but that it has become commonplace, politically-correct if you will, for law enforcement, the judicial system, educational institutions, city and various community leaders, not to mention the press, to so readily accept, and even pander and cater to and respond to the involvement of the NAACP and their accusations.

I recall a newspaper article, again in the Springfield News-Leader, that the local chapter of the NAACP was going to "study an incident" wherein it was alleged that a younger white man who worked at an auto repair shop might have made racial slurs toward an elderly black man who went to the shop seeking a $10 refund for a tire patch. Some sort of scuffle ensued and both men had minor injuries.

The article went on the say the local head of the NAACP was going to work with the group's state office and the Department of Justice to analyze information about the incident as a racially motivated assault. (over a $10 dollar tire patch?)

Now, the incident had been reported to the local sheriff's office, which had conducted an investigation, and referred it to the local prosecuting attorney. No charges were filed.

My question is—why wasn't that enough? Why was there a need to re-investigate the matter simply because the NAACP was crying foul? And why was all of this so important that it warranted its own story in the daily newspaper?

The fact of the matter is the NAACP puts its nose in the criminal justice system all the time, on behalf of blacks who they feel have been victims of crimes by whites that are either not prosecuted or not prosecuted severely enough (see the chapter herein on hate crimes) or where the blacks must surely be the victims of discrimination by white prosecutors who are being too tough in charging them as perpetrators of crimes.

And, again, the bad part of the NAACP becoming involved in these cases is that it's become too socially acceptable for law enforcement agencies, the court system, or the media, to give their rantings the time of day, to cow-tow to them so to speak, to pander to their cause.

Some law enforcement agencies, and prosecutors will actually re-open cases and conduct further investigations simply because the NAACP gets involved, and many times on cold, or very old cases in which a decision to not prosecute had already been made.

Why don't they re-investigate all cases? Why just the ones brought to their attention by the good old NAACP.?

Over and over, in papers all across America, almost daily, you read about instances such as this. And time and time again, local governments and the media succumb to the pressure of the group.

Power? You bet.

For another example of NAACP involvement in local communities, take the NAACP's involvement in Black Bike Week in Myrtle Beach, Sounth Carolina. They began to make their presence known there several years ago, and according to a report from Top Conservative News, their presence made the event more violent.

Over the years the NAACP sued the city. They sued local businesses. They got the city to force their officers to take 'cultural sensitivity' training.

Yet at the 2014 event, violence broke out and eight people were shot, three left dead. The report from Top Conservative News also claimed that the deaths became a national story but that the national media censored the name of the event, not calling it Black Bike Week in the stories reporting the violence and deaths.

Then in Ferguson, the NAACP made its presence known as well. They met with officials and law enforcement before the grand jury verdict came out. They had taken it upon themselves to 'shield' some of the actual witnesses who were going to testify in the grand jury proceedings.

The NAACP includes pages on their website with the heading, "Justice for Michael Brown."

And a fact I find interesting is the appearance of NAACP president Cornell Brooks on CNN Erin Burnett's Out Front program shortly after the verdict came out to downplay the, "Burn this bitch down," statements of Michael Brown's father Louis Head made just after the verdict was announced.

Burnett played the video showing his statements and asked Brooks if he felt that was a call for violence. Brooks said he did not feel the statement was a call for violence or that it caused any violence.

Then, after Burnett reminded him that Head, "was in a lot of pain" Brooks continued to deflect attention away from Head's rantings and went on a long rant himself excusing the alleged call for violence as insignificant to the entire Ferguson story.

Interesting, considering how many whites, myself included, see that ranting angry statement as the take away image of Ferguson for years to come.

Thugs being thugs, upset over the death of a felony-committing thug. (see the chapter on Ferguson)

And burn it did. This, a far cry from the peaceful non-violent methods of MLK and his followers.

But here was the head of the NAACP having his say on national television about the events in Ferguson.

Pandering for sure!

But the mere presence of, and almost always racial practices of the NAACP in society, and even their immense power isn't the only problem.

It's only a part of the problem.

The rest of the problem involves the fact that there isn't a National Association for the Advancement of WHITE People, or NAAWP.

In describing earlier how President George W. Bush had to find the leader of the NAACP when he was about to make one of his State of the Union addresses in order for a handshake, you will note I didn't describe how he also sought out the leader of the NAAWP.

That's because there isn't one.

And never will be.

Can you imagine just such a group? A group whose purpose it would be to promote the interests of white people in our society. A group whose members go around making sure that the status of white people in our society is preserved.

There to cry foul when a group of blacks assault a white person, calling on the legal system to label it a 'hate crime.' To speak out on behalf of whites who lost a job, or some other position to a black person who was less qualified than them because of affirmative action.

Dare we think that the leader of such a group could one day shake hands with an incoming president prior to his, or her, state of the union speech? And can you ever imagine that such a group's existence and their actions would become socially acceptable? It's almost funny to even think about, isn't it?

Black Pandering

In reality, a group such as that would immediately be labeled a white supremacist group and monitored by the Department of Justice, Homeland Security or whatever other government agencies exist for that purpose.

They would immediately be placed on every watch list out there, with perhaps a watch list being created just for them.

And that is true, even if the group had a vision statement similar to the NAACP, and did stand up for just and noble causes in society, the only difference being that they did it on behalf of whites.

But such a group, an NAAWP will never be allowed.

You know it and I know it.

End of story.

But why?

Why on the one hand do we have such a powerful racist group called the NAACP whose purposes and power are so readily and socially accepted, whose actions are feared by our leaders and press lest we find ourselves in their cross-hairs, yet find there is no place in society, for, nor will there ever be for a group called the NAAWP?

A politically-correct mindset of reverse discrimination perhaps?

Black pandering perhaps?

You will indeed see the NAACP referred to many times throughout this book, as they make their presence known in many areas of American life, and their influence, or meddling, depending on your viewpoint will be discussed in later chapters dealing with such hotbed racial issues as affirmative action, the Jena Six, racial profiling and hate crimes, among others.

As you read and see the countless references to the group herein, just keep in mind the tremendous power and influence of the NAACP, and wonder from time to time about the likewise obvious absence in society of my imaginary NAAWP, and how such a strong existence of the former weighed against the non-existence of the latter lends proof and credence to my proposition of the existence of a politically-correct mindset of reverse discrimination, and that blacks are pandered to in alarming proportions.

You might also begin to wonder what it would take to do away with this mindset, maybe even wonder whether it's possible at all, so that true equality of the races can finally begin to happen.

Chapter 4: Racial Profiling

The ticketing agent for the airline where Mohammed Atta, the leader of the September 11, 2001 attacks on the World Trade Center, and his companion, checked in for their fateful flight, has commented afterward on his first thoughts that day, "If this doesn't look like two Arab terrorists, I've never seen two Arab terrorists," in an interview on Paula Zahn Now on CNN in 2005.

We constantly see articles, newspaper stories, studies, reports of studies and various other printed and even video media about the subject of racial profiling.

And even though my opening example about the mastermind of 9/11 concerned Muslims, racial profiling usually is discussed in relations to blacks, and usually concerns allegations that blacks are being profiled, that is they are being specifically targeted and stopped by law enforcement officers more, and disproportionally more than whites.

Sometimes it concerns the disproportional number of blacks to whites, and other races, that are incarcerated in the nation's prisons and jails.

The United States Supreme Court decision that made racial profiling illegal was actually a decision that made it legal.

Let me explain.

In U.S. v Armstrong, in 1996, the Supreme Court actually ruled that racial profiling is constitutional, BUT only in the absence of specific proof that, "similarly situated" defendants of another race were disparately treated. Disparately treated means treated differently.

Got it?

And never has this been more talked about than during the recent unrest surrounding the results of grand jury rulings in the shooting death of teenager Michael Brown by officer Darren Wilson, which played out in the city of Ferguson, Missouri, a suburb of St. Louis, Missouri, (my home state, by the way) and the choke-hold death of Eric Garner by officer Daniel Pantaleo which occurred in Staten Island, New York City.

The deaths themselves, the grand jury results, the protests, and the national uproar which followed are covered in another chapter herein.

Racial profiling is the use of a person's race by law enforcement as a key ingredient in deciding whether to engage in law enforcement.

The national statistics available (and a better effort to gather, compile, and compare those statistics are a necessary ingredient to solving any racial profiling problem which exists) clearly show that blacks are stopped by law enforcement more than whites in almost all jurisdictions and further that blacks are incarcerated in most prisons and jails at a far larger percentage than whites.

The problem, and the fallacy of all racial profiling claims, is that the media and the writers of these articles, newspaper studies, and results of studies, at the point of seeing such 'alarming' numbers are too quick to automatically and immediately assume these numbers are the result and product of prejudice and discrimination, that racial profiling has and is occurring.

Further, society has become way too quick to allow this to happen, this being another area where the pandering of blacks is evident.

And all of a sudden, and constantly, law enforcement agencies everywhere and the justice system itself are disparaged for this racial profiling.

NAACP groups all over are demanding that law enforcement agencies and prison officials address this 'problem.'

The NAACP further says, in several articles on its web site, "More than 240 years of slavery and 90 years of legalized segregation in this country have created a legacy of racialized policing…"

In addition, one article on the NCAAP website entitled, 'Ferguson is Everytown, USA' cited, get this, a VIDEO GAME STUDY, which supposedly simulated the nearly instantaneous decisions made by police officers to shoot armed individuals and refrain from shooting the unarmed. According to the NCAAP, the study showed that participants were more likely to shoot black people than white people in error.

My only comment for that is, "Lock and Load!"

A video game?

On the NAACP's home page website for January 27, 2015, the second highlighted story (the first highlighted story was about the organization's 46th annual Image Awards.) is a report they are presenting entitled, "Born Suspect" and concerns 'stop and frisk' abuses and the group's continued fight to stop racial profiling in America.

The report includes an Anti-Racial Profiling Model Bill, a sample End Racial Profiling Act letter to Congress, Principles for an Effective Civilian Review Board, and a Police Misconduct Reporting Form.

Also included is a passionate plea, or call to action to its members, along with a social media campaign asking victims of racial profiling to share their stories.

I downloaded the report. It's 81 pages long.

Of course the report acknowledges the recent deaths of Michael Brown and Eric Garner in its introduction. The report calls racial profiling a "daily reality" with often "deadly consequences for communities of color…"

Barbara Bolling-Williams, Esq. the chairman of the Criminal Justice Committee for the Board of Directors of the group writes, "As leaders of the nation's largest and oldest civil rights organization, it is our goal to help end race-based discrimination, rooted in this nation's history of slavery and Jim Crow laws."

The report cited some statistics. According to the report 20 states do not have anti-racial profiling laws, leaving 30 that do. Eighteen states require mandatory collection of data and 18 states require the creation of commissions to investigate racial profiling allegations.

According to the report, the law enforcement community stepped up racial profiling after the attacks on the World Trade Center on September 11, 2001, "In fact, after the attacks, law enforcement….. relied heavily on the use of race, ethnicity, nationality, and religion to round up suspects in the name of the 'war on terror.'"

I, for one, am not so sure of this statement, at least as to race, or blacks. Perhaps it is true as to religious groups such as Muslims after 9/11.

I was also one of those who was asking the question during those years right after 9/11, "Well what is so bad about profiling?" I mean, it wasn't white middle class Americans who crashed airliners into the World Trade Center and Pentagon that day. It was jihadist, extremist Muslims, and yes, jihadist, extremist Muslims normally are the people who turn out to be the terrorists.

So why put a nation of 'free' people through all that rigorous screening at airports (and it got pretty bad, you gotta admit) when you can probably make a good guess about who the terrorists are?

And all of us, whether we realize it or not, profile on a daily basis. It's part of human nature. Take a clerk at a convenience store. He is not going to ask for ID on cigarette and alcohol purchases unless the person looks like (profiling) he or she might be too young.

An article in USA Today, dated November 19, 2014, right during the height of the Ferguson protests devoted almost a full page to the subject.

In the article, Brad Heath noted that the Ferguson Police department did proportionately stop blacks at a rate three times that of other races. Further, he found there were 1581 police departments across the USA which stopped black people at rates even greater than Ferguson.

And there were as many as 70 departments that arrested black people at a rate that was 10 times higher than whites, and the only reason the article suggested for that was racial profiling. (though he acknowledged, in one sentence, it might also be a byproduct of economic and educational gaps that exist)

He even cited various racial profiling "experts" to support his article.

Another article, by Emily Badger, in the Washington Post from April 30, 2014 entitled, 'Why it's so hard to study racial profiling by police,' indicted that according to a study cited by Attorney General Eric Holder, that by age 23, half of all black men have been arrested at least once, and that black men are six times more likely to be incarcerated than whites.

The article by Badger also referred to the New York Civil Liberties Union graph from 2011 which showed that in the NYPD's 'stop-and-frisk' program, 87 percent of those stopped were either black or latino.

The problem I have with the racial profiling debate, and the part which proves the existence of a politically-correct mindset of reverse discrimination is that ALWAYS missing from the racial profiling analysis is the NOTION that maybe, just maybe, blacks are committing more crimes than whites.

You never see this notion, not in Heath's article in USA Today or any of the other multitude of articles which address the subject.

Never.

Now to be fair, perhaps it could be said that Heath was alluding to it in a roundabout way by his one sentence that the disproportional numbers could be the byproduct of economic and educational gaps.

But hey, don't just allude to it. Talk about it!

I suggest he may be right. The disproportional numbers may, "be the byproduct of economic and educational gaps." But go on Mr. Heath and add the rest—"and because of these economic and educational gaps disproportional numbers of blacks are turning to crime!"

Why not acknowledge some of the statistics? Acknowledge the fact that in America approximately one half of all murders each year are committed by blacks, some of the more recent figures being 53.1 percent of ALL murders were committed by blacks, at least according to the FBI's Uniform Crime Report for the year 2010. According to the same report for the year 2011, the percentage of murders committed by blacks was 49.4 percent.

And these high percentages of murders were committed by blacks when blacks comprised only about 13 percent of the American population!

Could my notion that blacks simply commit more crimes be true?

I suggest so.

And why doesn't the racial profiling debates, articles, etc., ever mention this possibility? Black pandering and the politically-correct mindset of reverse discrimination are probably the answer.

The NAACP report which was cited earlier failed to mention the notion that perhaps blacks are just committing more crimes in all of its 81 pages!

Nothing.

Talk about that, NAACP.

Recognize that possiblility and ask if that could be the true answer to why blacks are jailed more.

Were the police correct?

Don't you think it might be a good idea to find out before jumping on the 'racial profiling' bandwagon?

But the NAACP doesn't want to touch that.

No one does.

Society doesn't let us because of the politically-correct mindset of reverse discrimination and the fact that our society and media pander to blacks.

One of the best ways I found to explain my point is to look at it from a different angle.

I'm sure you have had the opportunity to watch an NBA or college basketball game. Turn one on some afternoon, any game, I don't care, and do something for me.

Count the number of white players and compare it to the number of blacks ones. What was it 80 percent black on the floor at any given time? Perhaps 90 percent? Maybe even 100 percent, meaning all the players were black?

Does society allow us to assume that the white players are obviously being discriminated against because there are fewer of them out there?

Hell no.

Does that mean we are profiling basketball players by race?

Hardly.

Rather, it's just assumed by society that the black players are simply better players than the whites, more talented, and therefore out on the court at a percentage hugely disproportionate to whites. This is assumed and not even a question arises.

So why is the same rationale not allowed to explain why blacks occupy the nation's jails and prisons at a higher rate than whites and why blacks are stopped at a higher rate than whites by law enforcement agencies?

Shouldn't society be allowed to equally assume that blacks are there (in jail/on the court) simply because they (commit more crimes/are more talented) than whites? Instead, this same logic is never allowed.

Nothing on the NAACP website referred to above, or in the articles cited, mentions this possibility at all.

And article after article, newspaper report after newspaper report, study after study, cry foul, and give it a cute-sounding socially accepted label—racial profiling.

Shame on us all!

Even President Obama has seemed to allow the hollarings of racial profiling to fester by his own statements and the actions of his administration in response to Ferguson.

In an interview with the Huffington Post on Dec 17, 2014 he indicated it was common for black men to understand what it was like to be racially profiled. And that, "there's no black male my age who. . . hasn't come out of a restaurant and been waiting for their car and somebody didn't hand them their car keys."

First lady Michelle Obama mentioned a time when the President was asked to get coffee (assumed he was a waiter) for another guest at a black tie dinner., adding further that before he was President he was a black man from south Chicago who had trouble catching cabs.

Further, his administration, in announcing plans to conduct its own federal investigation into the deaths of Michael Brown and Eric Garner, (which again are covered in another chapter herein), and in essence questioning the results of the grand jury verdicts and placing a question on the very integrity of our judicial system concerning the "problem" of racial profiling as it relates to these two deaths gives support for my notion of a politically-correct mindset of reverse discrimination.

Again, why is society just allowed to assume there was racial profiling and hence, discrimination in these cases?

Even further, and a notion which I consider utterly absurd, is the recently floated idea of "unconscious bias" among our nation's criminal justice system as it relates to racial profiling, the most noted proponent of its existence being Attorney General Eric Holder.

In supporting and speaking to the Department of Justice's recent strengthening of the banning of federal law enforcement from profiling on the basis of national origin, religion and race, Holder spoke to the efforts to root out and eliminate what he calls the "unconscious bias" of police officers, according to Paul Sperry in an article in the New York Post.

According to Sperry, Holder's DOJ had more than doubled the number of police department probes compared with the last five years and pressured as many as fifteen, "consent orders" to stop biased policing.

In Seattle for instance, the feds based their findings of a "pattern and practice" of the Seattle police department of discrimination toward blacks, largely on "implicit bias" arguing cops "subconsciously" discriminated by making "disproportionate stops of non-whites." "Biased policing," explained the DOJ was not "primarily about the ill-intentioned officer, but rather the officer who engages in discriminatory practices subconsciously."

All of this, mind you, with the DOJ admitting it was unable to verify the accuracy of the complaints, and having never obtained the cops' side of the story in Seattle.

Are you kidding me? They can't PROVE actual bias and profiling, so they will simply ASSUME that officers are biased anyway, or, subconsciously?

In other words, police officers are biased and discriminated against blacks even where they didn't intend to, simply because the numbers show blacks were stopped more than whites?

And obviously no mention, not even close, of the notion that perhaps, just perhaps, blacks were stopped more because they were actually committing more crimes.

And yet society so readily eats this stuff up, pandering to the claims of blacks, adding to my notion of a mindset of reverse discrimination.

Now the idea of subconscious bias as it relates to racial profiling is not totally new. It reared its ugly head back in the July 16, 2009 arrest of black Harvard professor Henry Louis Gates by white police officer Sargent James Crowley of the Cambridge Police Department.

The officer, who had trained police in race relations, was accused of discrimination on the basis of his 'subconscious bias,' that he should have recognized the Mr. Gates was not a black thug criminal but that his subconscious led him to that conclusion anyway.

Never mind that the actions of Gates in attempting to re-enter his locked home (he had just returned from a trip and didn't have a key and was attempting to pry the door open, the same being seen by a neighbor and reported to 911 as an attempted burglary) had the appearance that he was, in FACT, a thug criminal or burglar.

He was arrested by Crowley with charges later being dropped. Crowley was accused of racial profiling.

Black Pandering

President Obama didn't help matters and actually stirred the pot by saying that, "what I think we know separate and apart from this incident is that there is a long history in this country of African Americans.......... being stopped by law enforcement disproportionally."

Obama later apologized for his comments and invited both parties to the White House to discuss the incident over beer in what has jokingly been referred to as the' Beer Summit.'

You might wonder how my notion of blacks simply committing more crimes could be tested.

Easy.

Just let any discussion on racial profiling and the numbers and comparisons of stops of blacks to whites be followed up with a simple question--What is the percentage of those black arrests which are actually convicted, or guilty of crimes?

You never, ever, see this question asked, much less answered, in any discussions on racial profiling.

Because if the percentage of actual convictions for black arrests is similar to the percentage of convictions for white arrests then guess what?

Racial profiling does not exist.

And my notion that blacks are just committing more crimes would appear to be true.

I can venture a guess.

My guess would be that the percentages of actual convictions for these black arrests is similar as for white arrests. And I volunteer that the larger numbers of blacks in prison compared to whites helps to support this guess.

What do you think?

The funny thing is that the studies and articles and newspaper reports that deal with racial profiling could easily include such a question and the answers to it. However, they never will.

And the reason?

Because society continues to pander to blacks, and allows the assumption that blacks are being profile, discriminated against by our 'white' criminal justice system, based on the existence of my politically-correct mindset of reverse discrimination.

Chapter 5: The Jena Six

Perhaps never before, until the last several years, has the back and forth of racial tensions played out on the public stage, with black pandering being so evident as with the incident which has come to be known as the Jena Six.

And perhaps there's no better example than the Jena Six for me to point out the premise of this book, that of a politically-correct mindset of reverse discrimination exists, as with an explanation of the facts thereof.

Jena, Louisiana has a population of about 3400 people. But this small town in the middle of Louisiana became the center of the nation's racial attention in 2006-2007 when a series of incidents involving black and white students from the town's high school became national news.

I visited Jena during the last days of writing this book. It was a sleepy little town on February 6, 2015, not unlike many other small towns I know of, including my own.

I felt it somewhat ironic as I drove past empty cotton fields in the Mississippi flatland coming out of Natchez, Mississippi.

I wondered if Jena sat upon these flats, and if that maybe served as a reminder of the brutal days of slavery and contributed to the racially charged story of the Jena Six.

It didn't.

Instead, Jena was in the foothills in the midst of pine trees. A lovely little town.

I, for one, was glad.

But even though Jena wasn't amongst the cotton fields, perhaps it was still too close, for the story of the Jena Six became the biggest story about race during the first decade of the 21st century.

Here are some photographs I took of Jena and the Jena High School where the major parts of the story of the Jena Six took place:

Six black teenagers (Robert Bailey, Mychal Bell, Carwin Jones, Bryant Purvis, Jesse Ray Beard, and Theo Shaw) were convicted for the beating of a white teenager, Justin Baker in December of 2006.

It was alleged by racial commentators and most of the national media that there was racial injustice in the convictions, in that the black teenagers were charged too seriously for the allegations and had been treated unfairly. The six blacks were dubbed the, "Jena Six."

A true understanding of the incident requires a presentation and understanding of the series of facts that led up to these claims. Clearly, the series of events in the days and months preceding the assaults were an escalation of racial tensions in the school and community.

The high school had a makeup of approximately 10 percent black to 90 percent white. Apparently, the black students routinely sat on some bleachers near the auditorium of the school, while the white students typically sat under a large tree in the center of the courtyard, which became referred to the 'white tree.'

In August of 2006, after an assembly, a black student inquired of the principal if the black students could sit under the tree. He reportedly told the black student that the blacks could sit wherever they wanted.

So they sat under the tree.

The next day, nooses were hanging from the tree. Three white students were reportedly responsible for the nooses.

In school disciplinary proceedings the principal recommended the white students be expelled for such behavior, but the school board overruled their expulsion.

The three students ended up spending time in an intermediate school, spent some time in in-school suspension and were referred to Discipline Court, among other sanctions.

Supposedly, the school superintendent downplayed the nooses, saying that he didn't think the nooses were any kind of a threat.

After the nooses, and arguments from various parties that the punishments for the hanging of the nooses was too minimal, (they argued that the students should have been expelled from school) the main high school building was destroyed by arson, this on November 30, 2006

Then on December 1, 2006, a fight broke out at a party, not on school grounds, where Bailey and four other black students showed up and were told they could not attend.

The very next day an incident occurred at a convenience store involving differing allegations between Bailey and three black youths and a white teenager named Matt Windham. Apparently Windham confronted the blacks with a gun, and Bailey was able to wrestle it away. (Bailer was later charged with this incident)

While no one is exactly sure what specifically led to the assaults in question (the local media felt that the burning of the school was the racially charged event that contributed the most) on December 4, 2006 the stage was set for the incident at the 'white tree.'

The six black students confronted Barker at the 'white tree.' Barker was punched, kicked and stomped by the six black teenagers. He suffered a concussion, and multiple bruises.

Some of the blacks initially said that Barker had told a racist joke, then later changed their story and said their actions were in response to the three nooses. But whatever the actual reasons, be it a racial joke, the nooses, or the fire, the motive for the assaults was clearly and undisputedly racial. (Can you say 'hate' crime 101?)

Again, I repeat, the motive was clearly and undisputedly racial.

. Interesting to note, and this is the part of this story that proves my notion of a mindset of reverse discrimination, is that the U.S. Attorney Donald Washington, indicated that the FBI investigation found that the hanging of the nooses was the only act of the entire Jena story which, "had all the markings of a hate crime." It wasn't prosecuted as such because such crimes committed by juveniles were rarely prosecuted in the federal.

Why not the assaults? Or at least I am wondering that.

There WAS a 'hate' crime filed in an incident that WAS related to the Jena Six which occurred about the same time.

Jeremiah Munsen, 19, who is white, was charged and plead guilty to a 'hate' crime for hanging a noose out of the back of his pickup and driving by protestors at a bus depot in Alexandria, Louisiana, which is about 35 miles from Jena.

The protestors were from Tennessee and awaiting a bus for home, after participating in the demonstrations for the Jena Six.

For his 'hate' crime Munsen was sentenced to four months in prison and had to serve a year of supervised release along with community service.

According to the Department of Justice, Munsen admitted that, "he and the other person had previously discussed the Ku Klux Klan and how they thought the Klan would have responded to the rally in Jena."

According to an opinion article by Mark Potok, Luke Visconti, Barbara Frankel, and Nigel Holmes, in the New York Times on November 25, 2007, after the big demonstration and rally in Jena on September 20, 2007, there was a rash of noose incidents, perhaps as many as 50-60. The article reminded readers that there were approximately 4700 lynchings from the 1880's through the 1960's.

The article suggested that instead of a, "renewed march toward racial and social justice…" that the rally in Jena might have caused a, "…. surprisingly broad and deep backlash against the gains of black America."

My question is, and I must refer you to the chapter herein on 'hate' crimes for a full discussion of the definition of such crimes, is how can the hanging of the nooses, be it at the 'white tree' or out of the back of a pickup, be a 'hate' crime but not the actual assaults of the white student by the blacks?

It's clearly an undisputed fact, according to the admissions by the black teenagers, that the assaults were motivated by race and race alone?

As such, those assaults meet the factual definition of 'hate crime' as clearly as any ever could. That's simply and easily Hate Crimes 101!

Yet not one mention was made by anyone concerning the Jena Six incident of those assaults being treated as such.

Just the nooses.

But why?

The only logical conclusion is that society and the media were so ingrained with the politically-correct mindset of reverse discrimination in 2006-07, that the incident in Jena would only BE allowed to be looked at from the angle of whites discriminating against blacks.

Thus, the nooses were magnified in the media and across the airwaves, because the presumption was allowed that a white Southern judicial system was surely discriminating against the black teenagers and punishing the blacks too severely for the assaults.

And not only were the assaults not even considered as 'hate' crimes with their more severe punishment, but were actually prosecuted to a much smaller degree than 'hate crime' status.

Should not society be asking my question? Or can 'hate' crimes only be used for crimes of white against black?

My notion of a politically-correct mindset of reverse discrimination and the pandering to blacks who cry racism, is the only thing that can explain this dilemma which existed in Jena.

Black Pandering

Even though coverage of this incident was at first only local, it quickly ballooned to national prominence. Al Sharpton and Jesse Jackson came running. Then the national media.

First on the national scene was the Chicago Tribune. Later CNN. Then others. Then the rest, or so it seemed.

Most, if not all of the media were questioning it from the too severe/racial injustice angle, falling right in line with, or rather being led like sheep down the same reverse discrimination road!

Calls were made from editorials and columnists for a renewed civil rights movement.

A huge pro Jena Six rally was held in Jena on September 20, 2007. Approximately 20,000 showed up along with the likes of Jesse Jackson, Al Sharpton, Martin Luther King III and musicians Ice Cube, Mos Def and Salt-N-Pepa.

A keynote speaker, Darryl Matthews, stated, "It is sobering to know that in 2007, Martin Luther King's dream of equal treatment, respect, fairness, and opportunity is still not realized."

Songs were released by prominent artists about the Jena Six, including John Mellencamp's "Jena" with lyrics, "Jena, take your nooses down."

How about a song entitled, "Blacks, quit assaulting people over race!"

Many major editorial columnists and editorial pages were sympathetic to the Jena Six and used the case to discuss broader trends of racism in the U S. criminal justice system and called for a renewed civil rights movement.

CNN, of course, ran interviews of the parents of the Jena Six and other residents of the town.

Of particular interest is how Democracy Now, which calls itself an independent global news hour reported the story in a video report.

Anchor Amy Goodman begins by telling how Jena, Louisiana had become the focal point in the debate around issues of race and the justice system in the U.S.

She described how the black teens had been charged with second degree murder and conspiracy and could face up to 100 years in prison without parole.

She also reported that one of the teens, Mychal Bell, had just been tried and an "all-white" jury took only two days to convict him (again, his charges were later reduced to juvenile crimes and he was sentenced to time he had served in the juvenile center) and he faced up to 22 years in prison.

This was said while the pictures of the six black teens were flashed on the screen. All smiling, in street clothes. No mug shots. No orange. Just six innocent looking, smiling, teens.

The story then shifted to an on-site reporter in Jena who interviewed one of the Jena Six, Jesse Beard, and described how he, "took us to where the nooses were hung," as pictures of the limbs of the tree were shown up close, swaying in the breeze.

She also had another one of the Jena Six, Robert Bailey, describe his reaction when he first saw the nooses, "It was an early morning. I seen em hanging. I was thinking the KKK hang nooses. They wanna hang somebody."

He added that people commit pranks but that nooses, "ain't no prank."

The story went on to explain how the administration had treated the nooses as a prank and only suspended the students who hung the nooses for three days, and how the parents of the black students were never even told about the noose incident.

Bailey's mother was quoted as being shocked that she didn't know or receive any notice about the nooses.

But why would she have even received any notice of the nooses? The assaults had not even been committed yet. So how would the school even know to give her a notice?

Nonetheless, she was asked about the meaning of the nooses and said, "It meant hatred."

I think you can get the gist of where the story was going, clearly to the side of – well here we are with yet another national incident where blacks had been discriminated against by whites.

Talk about black pandering!

Not once did the story contain a picture of a smiling Justin Barker, describing him as the victim of the assault. There were no pictures of the blood on the ground or his mangled condition.

In fact, the story presented no picture of Barker at all, and downplayed his injuries saying he was taken to a hospital but released and that he attended a school function later on that night.

Gosh, clearly the story was only a story about the nooses, not the assault, and how the black teenagers were being mistreated by the system.

The story even made it appear, or at least suggested, that the nooses were justification for the assaults.

A mindset of reverse discrimination?

Go look up the story and decide for yourself.

Petitions were circulated by various groups calling for reactions in response to the Jena Six case. The group Color of Change raised over $200,000 for the legal defense fund for the Jena Six.

And of course the NAACP used the incident to raise money as well, though they were criticized for using the incident to raise money for themselves and not for the Jena Six.

Pressure was put on the United States Department of Justice, by Representative John Conyers of the House Judiciary Committee to take some sort of action on the "miscarriages of justice that occurred in Jena, Louisiana."

Representative Sheila Jackson Lee and other members of the Congressional Black Caucus (funny, but I don't think we even have a Congressional White Caucus) made a plea to the Louisiana Governor to pardon the Jena Six, though Governor Kathleen Blanco refused to do so.

Many were calling on District Attorney Reed Walters to drop all the charges.

As a result of the public outcry, Bell, who was initially charged as an adult, was later to be retried as a juvenile, and ending up pleading to a reduced charge of battery and sentenced to credit for time served.

The other defendants ended up pleading no contest to simple battery and were fined $500 after a period of time where pressure was put on the judge to recuse himself for allegedly making questionable comments about the defendants.

There were, of course, no discussions that the assaults by the blacks against the white student be treated as 'hate crimes,' except in perhaps the most conservative of circles.

By and large it seemed there was a renewal, or at least a major upheaval calling for a renewal, of the civil rights movement. Included was a call for those whites responsible for the nooses being hung from the tree being charged with 'hate' crimes.

In addition, there were several noose incidents, as many as 60, following Jena, and perhaps in response to Jena which were also discussed with 'hate' crime language.

Seriously?

How in the world could people, be it media, celebrities or individuals be discussing the nooses as 'hate crimes' but clearly leaving out the assault by the black teenagers on the white student which was clearly, and admittedly, racially motivated?

How you ask?

Simply because of the existence of the politically-correct mindset of reverse discrimination and black pandering that is so clearly exhibited by the discussion of the Jena Six!

Politically-correct?

Yes.

But don't take it from me.

Take it from none other than Mark Potok, who is a staff director at the Southern Poverty Law Center, which is a black organization that tracks 'hate' crimes and 'hate' groups, and who was mentioned for co-authoring an article referred to above.

Potok, in an entirely different article, entitled, 'Hanging Hate' published on the website "In These Times" first made a statement about nooses, "What the nooses represent is a wider and deeper backlash by whites than people recognize."

But then he added this jewel, "White people think the events in Jena were whitewashed by an evil and politically correct press."

Yes, Mr. Potok we do!

And I couldn't have said it better myself!

Chapter 6: Hate Crimes

Perhaps these should more appropriately be called, "crimes committed by whites against blacks where we want to punish whites above and beyond the usual punishment because of all those years of slavery"

I know this sounds facetious, but we need only look at the history of these so-called 'hate' crimes together with the history of their application to see that 'hate' crimes are basically a one-sided joke, meaning they seem to be predominantly used against whites for crimes against blacks, and are brought about by the pressure on the judicial system by blacks over the years to get society to pander to them under the guise of discrimination.

The Department of Justice defines 'hate' crimes as, "the violence of intolerance and bigotry, intended to hurt and intimidate someone because of their race, ethnicity, national origin, religion, sexual orientation, or disability."

Clearly, anti-black bias, or crimes against blacks, is the most frequently reported 'hate' crime motivation in the United States.

Of the 8,208 'hate' crimes reported to the FBI in 2010, 48 percent were race-related, with 70 percent of those having anti-black bias, or committed by whites against blacks.

Seventy percent?

Or take the statistics from 2014, also brought to you by the FBI. In 2014 the number of 'hate' crimes reported was down, to 5928 incidents. Of those 48.5 percent were racially motivated. And of those racially-motivated 'hate' crimes, 66 percent had an anti-black bias, while 21.4 percent had an anti-white bias.

Check any year.

The numbers fluctuate some, but the percentages stay roughly the same.

In other words, 'hate' crimes are primarily used in crimes committed by whites against blacks. Period.

Now, quickly refer back to the chapter on the Jena Six and recall the facts.

As you remember, six black students assaulted the white student because of several incidents that happened concerning the 'white tree' which was a tree in the schoolyard where the white students typically hung out.

A black student asked the principal if he could sit under the white tree and was told he could sit anywhere he liked.

However, the next day, nooses were hanging from the 'white tree.' Because of the nooses, and possibly also because of some other incidents that had occurred, all of which were admitted to as racial, (i.e. because of race and only because of race, which is the textbook definition of a 'hate' crime) six black students assaulted a white student under the 'white tree.'

They were charged and convicted.

But were the assaults looked at as a 'hate' crime?

Not even close. In fact, the feds ONLY considered the acts of the three whites who hung the nooses from the tree as having the, "markings of a 'hate' crime," even though they were not charged as such because they were juveniles.

Now, another student WAS charged with a 'hate' crime for hanging a noose from the back of his pickup in front of some of the Jena Six protestors. He spent four months in jail.

Further, and instead of being looked at as 'hate' crimes, the convictions of the six black students were attacked as being too excessive, and their charges reduced to almost nothing.

Black Pandering

The white judicial system of the rural southern Louisiana town of Jena was discriminating against the blacks, or so it was claimed, and allowed to be presumed by society.

The pandering of blacks train was leaving the station and picking up steam!

Even in the shooting death of Michael Brown in Ferguson, and the chokehold death of Eric Garner in Staten Island, New York, there were rumblings of 'hate' crime language and accusations against the white officers involved in each of the deaths.

I remember watching with my own eyes, and perhaps you saw it too, as Michael Brown's step father Louis Head jumped up on a platform with Michael Brown's mother, his wife, after the grand jury decision to not indict officer Darren Wilson, and began angrily inciting the crowd to, "burn this bitch down."

Over and over, in an angry tone and manner, "burn this bitch down."

Now, we've got to ask--why wasn't that prosecuted as a 'hate' crime?

The reason for his rant was clearly racial. In fact, everything about Ferguson was racial. Right from the start.

I guess we don' know if his words were directly heard by the crowd or any of the potential rioters who later started the fires.

But, by the end of the next day, some 20-25 fires had destroyed millions of dollars of Ferguson businesses and properties and I suppose it could be said that, "the bitch had been burnt to the ground!"

But to my knowledge, no one seriously considered charging Head with so much of a crime, much less a 'hate' crime.

In addition, shortly after Ferguson, a video taken on a phone by on onlooker went viral on the internet showing a black teen viciously assaulting a white person on a commuter train, or bus, in St. Louis, immediately after he had asked the white person what he thought of the Michael Brown situation, and got no response. As aggressive as the assault was nothing at all was talked about it being a 'hate' crime even though, once again, the criteria for it being considered as such was clearly met. In black and white!

And do you remember all of the assaults committed by blacks against whites after the George Zimmerman verdict for the shooting death of Trayvon Martin?

Such assaults were committed all across the country and usually accompanied by language or slogans along the lines of, "that's for Trayvon," or, "remember Trayvon."

I don't know how an assault could fit the definition of a 'hate' crime any better than these. But we never heard about any of these being looked at as 'hate' crimes. Not even close.

It just goes to show how far the pendulum has swung away from 'equality' in how the races are treated by the justice system in our society, at least as to the application of 'hate' crimes.

A mindset of reverse discrimination?

Black pandering?

You bet.

Here's another little test for you to gauge for yourself if I am not correct in this assessment of 'hate' crimes.

Take a look at the FBI's website and specifically the page on 'hate' crimes.

There is a picture at the top. What do you see?

As I look at it while writing this page (January 15, 2015) it is a picture of the Ku Klux Klan, dressed in their white hooded robes and burning a cross. What kind of 'hate' crime is that picture referring to?

Do you think it refers to a black against white 'hate' crime?

No way, and exactly the opposite for sure.

In fact the heading on the page talks about the beginning of the use of the term, 'hate' crimes being in the 1980's in references to the Skinheads (the same being white, whose philosophy was clearly anti-black) and the beginning of the FBI's investigating ' hate' crimes being after World War II and the emergence of the Ku Klux Klan, again concerning white against black crimes.

This, together with the mindset of society of automatically assuming that blacks are being discriminated against by whites, and no wonder that almost 70 percent of all 'hate' crimes being investigated are for crimes committed by whites against blacks.

It's seems as if blacks cannot commit a 'hate' crime against whites.

Even the latest FBI statistics available (for 2012) show 66.6 percent of the racially motivated 'hate' crimes were anti-black whereas only 22.4 percent were for anti-white bias.

Sad.

The website further references convictions for the hanging of the noose as a 'hate' crime, although it doesn't say exactly how many of the 'hate' crimes in the statistics were specifically for the hanging of a noose.

An article way back in the Washington Post in November of 2007 concerning 'hate' crimes and the increase of the same after the Jena Six incidents in 2006-2007, indicated that the FBI does NOT break out 'noose' incidents in the reporting of 'hate' crimes.

Why not?

That would be easy and simple, don't you think?

I do.

The Department of Justice's very own press release labeled 'Fact Sheet" from Thursday, November 15, 2007 reported that from fiscal year 2001 to fiscal year 2007, the Department of Justice had charged 62 defendants in 41 CROSS-BURNING incidents.

Cross-burning is a 'hate' crime too?

I suppose it's easier to count crosses on fire than it is to count 'nooses.'

So one has to wonder why the FBI is not keeping track of the number of 'noose' incidents, especially when the Department of Justice, in the same article, specifically stated, "a noose is a powerful symbol of hate and racially motivated violence," recalling the days of lynching of blacks.

The article further noted that the Department of Justice was actively investigating a number of noose incidents at schools, workplaces, and neighborhoods around the country after Jena.

How about the giving of the Black Panther salute? I wonder if that has ever been charged as a 'hate' crime.

I couldn't find it in the FBI website as such, although I could venture a guess.

A good question to be asked is how is the hanging of the noose a 'hate' crime and the giving of the Black Panther salute not?

Couldn't it be argued that both are merely an expression of free speech under the U.S. Constitution?

To be fair, I also did not see where the flying of the Confederate flag was a 'hate' crime in and of itself, but countless articles abound concerning those who want to make its flying a 'hate' crime.

And I suppose if one is going to look at 'hate' crimes, then one should also look at groups which have been labeled 'hate' groups. Of course some of one's analysis on 'hate' groups might depend somewhat on who is doing the labeling as well.

Start with the Southern Poverty Law Center.

If you didn't already know you probably should know that the Southern Poverty Law Center is basically a black organization.

The Southern Poverty Law Center currently lists 939 'hate' groups, and at the top of their list are neo-Nazis, Klansmen, white nationalists, neo-confederates, and racist skinheads, all groups that one could have probably predicted would be on the Southern Poverty Law Center list.

As you might be able to predict, from the makeup of the group doing the labeling, most of the groups on the list are white!

Also interesting is the inclusion in the Southern Poverty Law Center's list of 'hate' groups such as America's Promise Keepers, The American Family Association, The California Coalition for Immigration Reform, and The Federation for American Immigration Reform.

The first two of those just mentioned are Christian groups that to my knowledge are well respected, while the later are simply immigration reform groups.

I am not sure having desires for immigration reform should land one on a 'hate' group. If so does that mean that George W. Bush and John McCain, and even President Obama should be included on some 'hate' list since they all favor some sort of immigration reform?

Further, I scanned the list under the Black Separatist Group category, and saw the New Black Panther Party and something called the Black Riders Liberation Party as the only 'true' black groups on the list.

I say the only 'true' black groups because the Southern Poverty Law Center's list also lumped The Nation of Islam and The Israelite Church of God in Jesus Christ into this 'black' group category.

I guess the Southern Poverty Law Center was afraid their list of Black Separatist 'hate' Groups was looking a little too scant, compared to the other 937 'hate' groups, most of which were white!

As you can see, deciding just who the 'haters' are kind of depends on who is doing the deciding, as it's apparent that some group's lists might be somewhat one-sided.

And because of this, it looks like any attempt to rely on any 'hate' list might not contribute anything meaningful to a truly intelligent study of 'hate' in America.

As you can see, by the numbers and statistics presented, and by the total bias of at least one of the groups who is trying to be the decider of who the 'haters' are, blacks are clearly being pandered to, and whites are clearly being discriminated against, in the application of 'hate' crime investigations and prosecutions.

Further, the extremely disproportionate way in which 'hate' crimes are applied to crimes committed by whites against blacks, versus crimes committed by blacks against whites, is just further proof of the politically-correct mindset of reverse discrimination.

And because of this extreme disparity, and the degree to which the mindset of reverse discrimination appears to have rooted itself in the analysis of 'hate' crimes, you might actually wonder if my somewhat humorous definition in the first paragraph of this chapter, that 'hate' crimes are crimes committed by whites against blacks where we want to punish the whites more because of all those years of slavery, might just have a hint of truth to it!

Chapter 7: Historically Black Colleges and Universities

Does society pander to blacks in the area of education? We need only to look at affirmative action (covered in another chapter herein) and colleges we call Historically Black Colleges and Universities to answer that question affirmatively.

In 1980 President Carter signed an executive order officially designating certain colleges and universities as "historically black colleges and universities" and established a federal program, "to overcome the effects of discriminatory treatment and to strengthen and expand the capacity of historically black colleges and universities to provide quality education."

In a presidential proclamation made at a reception at the White House observing Historically Black Colleges and Universities week in 2011, President Obama remarked, "HCBUs continue a proud tradition as vibrant centers as intellectual inquiry and engines of scientific discovery and innovation. New waves of students, faculty, and alumni are building on their rich legacies and helping America achieve our goal of once again leading the world in having the highest proportion of college graduates in the world by 2020,"

I guess the big question here is where are the presidential proclamations for Historically White Colleges and Universities week?

Oh wait, there isn't one because we don't have such a week, do we?

There is even something called the White House Initiative on Historically Black Colleges and Universities administered under the U.S. Department of Health, Education and Welfare's Office of Post Secondary Education.

Undue favor upon a particular minority group?

Is there a similar White House initiative for white ones?

Nope.

Today there are over one hundred historically black colleges and universities in the United States. Cheyney University in Pennsylvania was the first, established in 1837. Approximately 300,000 students attend these black colleges.

According to the U.S. Department of Education historically-black colleges and universities were established to, "serve the educational needs of black Americans."

There is nothing on the U.S. Department of Education website that says anything at all about there being any historically white colleges and universities to "serve the needs of white Americans."

In a working paper by Ford Foundation Senior Fellow Phillip L. Clay in 2011-2012 to the Ford Foundation, it was noted that HBCUs continue to play a critical role in "advancing the race."

What kind of statement is that in a world where the true goal should be for equality of the races? Does such a statement as that do anyone any good?

I submit not. It's just further proof that society panders to blacks.

But it was said, in a paper to the Ford Foundation no less.

Can you imagine me writing a statement about special treatment for white colleges and universities and how such treatment continues to play a critical role in "advancing the (white) race?"

How well would that go over?

Now I guess you could argue that people of any race, be it black, white, asian, hispanic, should be able to promote the advancement of theirs. The problem is that even though I might want to advance mine (white, in case you haven't already figured that out) I am not allowed to say it without it being looked at as racist, and that's anywhere, much less in a paper to the Ford Foundation.

And in this discrepancy is the very idea and proposition of this book, the existence of a politically correct mindset of reverse discrimination.

I went to the University of Missouri (go tigers!) back in the early 1980's. That is the largest and finest (I am biased) institution of higher education in Missouri, and perhaps one of the finest in the nation. (go tigers!)

ANY person of ANY race can apply for admission to attend college there, including black people.

So why do we continue to have in our society these historically black colleges and universities where the percentage of black students generally range from 85 to 90 percent

And why do the leaders of our nation, including the president himself, give such praise to the same, when their very existence, without a corresponding contingent of white colleges and universities clearly shows a pattern of obvious, but socially accepted, reverse discrimination?

When you look at the history of these colleges you see they came into existence primarily during the time when blacks were denied acceptance into public institutions. And as such, the creating of these colleges and universities for blacks did have merit.

But that was then.

That was before the civil rights movement and the desegregation of the public education system, for elementary, secondary, and higher education, brought about during the turbulent 1960's and 70's.

Famous cases before the U.S. Supreme Court such as Brown v. Board of Education in 1954 opened up enrollment for all races in our public educational system. Not to mention the changes in education brought about by the broad sweep of the Civil Right Act of 1964.

The playing field was leveled for all students, regardless of race, under this Act and by various cases in the courts defining the requirements of the act.

An additional response to these court cases and the Civil Rights Act of 1964 was that all institutions that received federal funding put in place various forms of affirmative action to increase their racial diversity.

In short, affirmative action, (which has a chapter herein all to itself) actually acted to artificially tilt the playing field in favor of minorities at these public institutions. It was imposed and reverse discrimination became actual law, if you will. Thousands and thousands of whites lost enrollment spots at colleges and universities across this country because of affirmative action.

It just follows that the very reasons for the setting up of these black colleges and universities ceased to exist with the advent of desegregation, and affirmative action, and in a truly racially equal society so should the very existence of the historically black colleges and universities themselves.

But because of the politically-correct mindset of reverse discrimination that also exists and the pandering to blacks that accompanies this mindset, these historically black colleges and universities not only continue to exist in our society, but to thrive, and continue to have favor in high places, along with the funding that goes with them.

One good question, given the desegregation of public education in America, is how is it even LEGAL for these historically black colleges and universities to continue to exist? Especially given their segregated identities and nature.

Existing is one thing, but government sanctioned?

The Adams v. Califano case in 1977 did somewhat deal with the issue. The U.S. Department of Health Education and Welfare was sued for enforcement violations of the Civil Rights Act.

It can be argued that this is the decision by a court that actually made reverse discrimination legal.

The court actually recognized the "unique role" of historically black colleges and universities in meeting the educational needs of black students.

A criteria was established to actually provide resources to these colleges while asking them to expand their non-minority enrollment, with a goal to allow them to retain or enhance their historic stature.

I'm not sure the request to expand non-minority enrollment was ever taken to heart as, again, the percentages of blacks at these historically black colleges and universities still averages about 85 to 90 percent.

Oddly enough, a major group of black educators, the National Association for Equal Opportunity in Higher Education, broke ranks with the NAACP in the Adams/Califano case, filing an amicus brief arguing that black institutions had NOT supported desegregation, probably based on the high percentages of blacks that most of these colleges still maintained.

So here was a black group admitting, essentially, that these colleges were discriminating against whites.

More recently, in 2009, a historically black college WAS hit with a reverse discrimination suit. Three white faculty members at Benedict College in South Carolina claimed they were passed over for jobs or let go because of their race.

The school responded through its attorney, "... that it embraces diversity and opposes discrimination..... Benedict College is an equal opportunity educational institution."

But according to its website, Benedict College is a private liberal arts college with, "a continued commitment to facilitate the empowerment, enrichment and full participation of African Americans in American society."

So which is it Benedict? Equal opportunity or enrichment of African Americans?

The lawsuit was settled with the college paying each of the faculty members $55,000, with the college denying liability but forking over the dough because it would cost that much or more to defend the lawsuit.

Darn lawyers! It would have been an interesting case to see how the college was going to walk that fine line of maintaining its historically black college status but proving it was an equal opportunity employer at the same time.

I wasn't able to find the exact percentages of black students or faculty at Benedict. But in looking up its website it featured photographs of the women's basketball team, the theatre ensemble, the women's cross country team, and the National Society of Collegiate Scholars inductees, among others and in these photographs mentioned there wasn't a single white person pictured.

None.

And in a picture of the winter graduating class from that year, there was not a single white person among at least 65 pictured.

Yep. Still black.

According to statistics, these black colleges have white student populations of only about 10 percent, and that is only because about half of these black colleges have been sued about their lack of diversity.

Question. How is only 10 percent white considered diverse?

Some added information is that Benedict College was the fifth-worst on Washington Monthly's list of "America's Worst Colleges," in 2014.

This is an index that factors graduation rates heavily into its indexing of colleges. And, when the focus of the list was changed to include degrees earned by part-time students, transfer students and students borrowing money, the college rose, to the top of the worst list.

The report including the list suggested it might be time to rethink the role historically black colleges and universities play, noting that these colleges struggle with (graduation) results.

What about federal funding you ask?

Title III of the Higher Education Act of 1965 authorizes specific funds for historically black colleges and universities.

The program even has a name. The "Strengthening Historically Black Colleges and Universities Program."

Oh yes, and another called the "Strengthening Historically Black Graduate Institutions Program."

I had never even heard of these until I began research for this book.

But they do exist and have existed for quite some time.

A question I have to ask is—why isn't special funding for these historically black colleges considered defacto reverse discrimination?

Isn't this pandering to a degree of giving preferential treatment to blacks?

Part B of the Higher Education Act of 1965 actually provides DIRECT funding for these colleges, designated as part B institutions, defined as, "any historically black college or university that was established prior to 1964, whose principal mission was, and IS (emphasis added) the education of black Americans..."

President Obama's 2011 budget included a $30 million funding increase for these institutions, to $279.9 million. The actual appropriation by your Congress was just $13 million less.

In 1975, Jake Ayers Sr. filed a lawsuit against the state of Mississippi for giving more financial support to its predominantly white colleges. (define that as colleges which were public and did accept blacks for enrollment)

The lawsuit was finally settled in 2002 by the state agreeing to direct $503 million to three historically black colleges over a 17 year period.

Also, the state of Georgia NAACP sued the state of Georgia in 2010 claiming it had systematically underfunded that state's three historically black colleges. Georgia NAACP Chapter president Edward Dubose stated, "we refuse to allow the demise of our historically black colleges."

Can you imagine there ever being a government designation for 'historically white colleges and universities,' with a purpose to strengthen and expand the educational opportunities of WHITE students?

I didn't think you could.

Yet article after article tells of the acceptance of the historically black ones and goes on and on about how these historically black colleges and universities are needed in our society.

And not only do these historically black colleges and universities continue to exist in large numbers way past the time when the reason for their existence is gone, they are also funded by the legislature, applauded and praised by the highest levels of the executive branch, and even declared 'legal' by the courts!

So in the field of education the politically-correct mindset of reverse discrimination I have identified is alive and kicking and doesn't appear about to change anytime soon!

Chapter 8: Reverse Discrimination in Sports and the Black Coaches Association

Did you ever watch a college or NBA basketball game and count the number of black players on the court at any given time? How about a college or NFL football game?

Watch any of those games and you will notice that about 80-90 percent of the players are black. It's even not unusual in some basketball games for EVERY player on the court to be black.

Now, have you ever heard anyone try to make the claim that white players must be discriminated against because there are so few of them out on the court or field? That it's racist?

I didn't think so.

I mean, the overall percentage of blacks in society is nowhere near 80-90 percent. (It's roughly 13 percent according to the United States Census Bureau.) So if there is that big of a percentage of black players and so few white ones, then surely this must be discrimination and racism.

Right?

Well society, by its actions, or rather inactions, answers that question with a profound NO. And the reason is it's automatically accepted, or assumed, that the black players are simply more talented than the white ones, or clearly have more athletic ability than the white ones. That's why there are more blacks than whites out on the court or field of play.

It's politically-correct in our society to reach that conclusion.

No one assumes anything different.

And even the story line of "White Men Can't Jump" revolves around that assumption.

All the black parking lot basketball players are just sure the goofy-looking clumsy white kid with his hat turned sideways, played by Woody Harrelson, cannot play basketball.

He's white! There's no way he can jump, run, or shoot as well as the black players. That's a given. So sure, they will take the bet from Wesley Snipes that they can win the game.

But smoked they get. For Harrelson turns out to be a basketball stud.

And thus, Snipes and Harrelson hustle the black players from the street in relying on this assumption. And everyone laughed. No one cried discrimination or racism.

Now, what about the ranks of coaches in college and professional basketball and football?

Most of those coaches happen to be white. Now there are some black coaches, and some who I might add are extremely successful. I personally have as much admiration for Tony Dungy (former coach of the Indianapolis Colts and now NBC commentator), as a coach AND as a person as about any white person I know.

But the percentage of black coaches for these sports, admittedly, is low.

So surely society can likewise accept that the reason for this is that the white coaches are simply more talented than the black ones. Right?

I mean, if blacks are more talented athletes, for whatever reason. (and you could argue about the reasons all day long) then it's perfectly alright to assume that whites are more talented at coaching, isn't it?

Well, that's where you're wrong.

For inherent in any discussion about coaching is the socially accepted assumption that there must be discrimination against blacks by the white hierarchy in college and professional sports as it relates to the hiring of black coaches.

And that is where the Black Coaches Association comes in, and the pandering to blacks is as evident in sports as in any other area of our society.

The Black Coaches Association (BCA) is the former, and more widely used name of a group now called the Black Coaches and Administrators (BCA). The change of the name was made in 2007.

The overall goal of the BCA, simply stated, is to get more black coaches hired in college and professional sports. The group was formed in 1988, with the nobly stated purpose to "enhance the employment opportunities and professional development of the ethnic minority professional."

First off, it's a little odd that the purpose seems to include all ethnic minorities while only the word 'black' is included in its title. But I will let you read into that whatever you will.

The Institute for Diversity and Ethics in Sports (TIDES) is a group that works with the BCA and researches and publishes a variety of studies including studies of racial attitudes in sports as well as something called the Racial and Gender Report Card, which is an assessment of hiring practices in professional and college sports coaching positions.

The report specifically analyzes, among other things, the hiring of ethnic minority coaches in Division I college football, excluding statistics from 'historically black colleges.'

Imagine that, and see the chapter herein on 'historically black colleges.' I suppose the inclusion of the number of black coaches at 'historically black colleges' would skew the numbers? Or perhaps if those numbers were included it might lead to a conclusion that there wasn't a problem at all?

The schools are actually graded from "A" to "F," on whether they hired a black coach or at least considered one.

In 2004 the association began using a five-part system to evaluate hiring practices in Division I-A football to serve, "as a cornerstone for accountability," according to executive director Floyd Keith, in a release on CBS Sportsline for October, 21, 2003.

The association was going to grade individual schools on the number of contacts made with the BCA's executive director, the percentage of minorities involved in the hiring process, the number of minority coaches interviewed, the length of time involved in the hiring process, and how the process compared to institutional affirmative action policies.

Seriously?

A college search committee is required to call the executive director of the Black Coaches Association before hiring a new head football coach? I wonder which white group they are likewise required to call?

This report card is published, (to the hilt), every year, and society in general and the sports world just seems to accept it in stride.

Can you say pandering?

References are routinely made that the college football head coaching position is emphatically the most segregated position in all of college sports.

Notice that society cannot just assume that more whites are hired to be head college football coaches simply because they are more talented than blacks and make better head coaches than blacks, even though this is the reasoning used, and accepted as politically-correct, as to why there are more black college and professional players in sports, particularly football and basketball.

The real power of the BCA is the extreme pressure they put on colleges and professional teams to adopt the hiring policies recommended, or demanded as the case may be, by the BCA. That and the immense negative publicity that can result if their recommendations are not followed.

Teams are literally bombarded with letters and calls, not to mention all of the mountains of publicity. Don't dare risk receiving an "F" grade in minority hiring practices and for this to be published for all the world to see.

It looks almost like a form of blackmail. Sign on with the BCA and abide by their demands lest you find yourselves the target of extreme negative publicity.

For example, in The Boulder Daily Camera on November 26, 2012, there was an article about how the executive director of the Black Coaches Association (I wonder why the old name of the organization was used) Floyd Keith said he was disappointed that the University of Colorado had fired coach John Embree, who was the first black head football coach in the school's history, after only two years.

This despite the fact that his team was 1-11 that season and only 4-21 for the last two seasons. The reasoning was that he thought he should have gotten at least three years at the helm.

The real problem I see is why was it even important that the head of the BCA had an opinion on the matter, that was considered to be newsworthy, but for the fact that it was a black coach getting fired.

I wonder how many similar times Mr Keith spoke up on behalf of white coaches who had been fired after only two years on the job? I don't know, but I bet I have a good guess.

Keith was also attributed in the article as saying that contacting the BCA for input was standard practice with any hire for football and basketball programs these days, and further that the numbers were still heavily skewed toward white coaches even though college rosters had included high percentages of black players for decades.

The BCA cites that from 1982 to 2011 there were 546 coaching jobs open for which 50 blacks were hired. That's 9.2 percent. Okay, so it' not equal to the roughly 13 percent number which is the overall percentage of blacks in the United States population. I wondered but didn't calculate what the percentage would be if it included the number of black coaches at the more than 100 'historically black colleges.'

One question might be, what number do they actually want to achieve? Would the BCA be satisfied if 13 percent of the coaches for these sports were black since this is the percentage of blacks in society? I am guessing that number would not make them happy. But that is just a guess!

The National Football League, or NFL has the "Rooney Rule" which requires teams to interview an African American candidate before hiring a coach. The rule was put in place in 2003 and also requires teams to interview minority candidates for positions for senior football operations.

There doesn't seem to be any requirements in this rule that teams must consider white candidates for the playing positions, lest there be a truly 'equal' playing field in sports. That would be racist.

Interesting to note is the fact that the Detroit Lions were fined $200,000 in 2003 for their failure to interview an African American candidate for their head coaching job, when Steve Mariucci was hired to replace Marty Mornhinweg without interviewing any other candidates.

Brian W. Collins, in a note in the New York University Law Review, June, 2007, argued that the pre-Rooney rule NFL hiring process, "remained relatively static because decision makers unwittingly held . . . archaic biases regarding the intellectual ability of minority candidates to handle the organizational complexity in football."

Shame on society and Mr. Collins for assuming that blacks have less intellectual capacity or are intellectually inferior to whites, right? That's discrimination.

But society CAN assume, and is allowed to assume, that whites have less athletic ability than blacks, as least as far as filling up the NBA, NFL, and NCAA major sports rosters.

For further proof of my claim, notice a statement by Collins in his note that, "Camouflaged by the racial composition of its athletes, (read that as, it's OK for there to be an abnormal percentage of black players) significant barriers persist in the industry's upper-management positions." (read that as there must be discrimination against blacks) He called it an 'unconscious bias.' Well thank you Mr. Collins. I would hate to think that such discrimination is intended!

Collins cited what he called 'overtly racist assertions' regarding the management abilities of African Americans which had been recorded in earlier years.

Los Angeles Dodgers executive Al Campanis had stated in 1987 that there were few African American baseball managers because, "African Americans may not have some of the necessities to be, let's say a field manager, or perhaps a general manager."

The Dodgers and MLB distanced themselves from the statement.

Then in 1992, (oddly the same year that, "White Men Can't Jump" came out and was NOT labeled as an 'overtly racist assertion' by Mr. Collins) Cincinnati Reds owner Marge Schott got into hot water with her statement that, "I once had a n------ work for me. . . I would never hire another n------. I'd rather have a trained monkey working for me than a n------."

She was suspended a year for her comments, and this at the exact same time people were plopping down money all over the country to laugh at Harrelson and Snipes and their antics in "White Men Can't Jump," with no one, including Mr. Collins, saying a thing about the movie and its blatant and obvious racism.

Reverse discrimination was clearly being played out big time in 1992!

And pandering to blacks was clearly evident in sports!

Collins further claimed that even though explicit assertions of African Americans intellectual inferiority, such as the statements of Campanis and Schott had waned, that many of those in the positions to hire head coaches continued to harbor similar stereotypes unconsciously."

Gosh, here was a guy telling people what they were thinking even when they didn't realize they were thinking it. Funny, he couldn't tell, or perhaps just didn't want to tell, what people were thinking when they assumed that whites were not as talented to play basketball as blacks.

Though he did state that, "people commonly attribute the success of African American athletes solely to natural ability," thus implying that he clearly bought into the socially-accepted assumption that blacks were simply more athletically talented than whites.

In short, the proposition of my book of the existence of a politically-correct mindset of reverse discrimination was made vivid by Collins explaining how he thought it was obviously discrimination against blacks by whites, based on his 'unconscious bias' theory as the reason for there being so few black coaches in the NFL, while at the same time not even approaching the idea that there could be any discrimination against whites as to the percentage of black players to white ones.

Even popular black attorney Johnnie Cochran (remember the O. J. Simpson trial?) along with attorney Cyrus Mehri published a report detailing the dismal record of minority hiring and threatened class action lawsuits against NFL franchises unless, "substantial progress was made by the NFL in the hiring of African Americans for head coaching positions."

Their report, in 2002, caused the NFL to hastily form the NFL Committee on Workplace Diversity, to promote diversity in coaching and management, which in turn led to the aforementioned Rooney rule.

I don't recall anyone ever threatening to sue the NFL or NBA for the lack of white players, do you?

You see, it's okay to assume discrimination of whites against blacks but never the opposite be true.

Factually, the percentage of black coaches in college and professional football and basketball is low, and the socially-accepted rationale seems to be that there must be discrimination.

The BCA perpetuates and thrives on this socially-accepted rationale even though they would probably argue that the hiring of coaches should be according to talent, or at least one would think it. Well on that I wholeheartedly agree.

But I have to question, why can't we just assume that the numbers already DO reflect the talent of the various coaching job applicants? I mean, if we so readily accept this assumption as to players, then why doesn't if follow that the same is true for coaches?

And the answer to that is once again my proposition of the existence of a politically-correct mindset of reverse discrimination in our society keeps the two assumptions apart.

And I guess that is really the heart of the matter. There is nothing in itself wrong for Mr. Collins to have argued discrimination in the hiring of black coaches in the NFL. Nor for the Black Coaches Association to strive to get more black coaches hired for college and professional football and basketball. Or even for the Rooney rule to force consideration in the hiring of blacks in the upper echelons of the NFL.

The wrong part is that discrimination of blacks by whites is automatically assumed as to coaches, WHEN there is no such assumption for discrimination of whites by blacks as to players.

For we do not have, and never will have a White Players Association whose goal it is to put pressure on college and professional teams to hire white players for the various playing positions on the court or field.

Can you imagine that? A group whose mission is to get 8 or 9 white players out on the basketball court at the same time (or a percentage roughly equal to the percentage of whites in society), arguing that there must be discrimination against white players because there are so few of them playing.

And what's more, could you ever see society accepting that reasoning?

I didn't think so.

Nor will there ever be a version of the Rooney rule that goes one step further, and requires that white players must be considered for every position on the football field or basketball court before any position is filled.

That would be labeled even more ludicrous, racist, and doomed from the start. There's no way that's going to happen.

Not with my politically-correct mindset of reverse discrimination so ingrained in our society and the degree to which this mindset allows black pandering.

And besides, remember, we can't jump!

Chapter 9: Black History Month and Harrison, Arkansas

Every President since 1976 has officially designated the month of February each year as Black History Month, or National African American History Month.

This grew out of Negro History Week, which was the idea of historian Carter G. Woodson and other prominent black leaders back in the early 1900's. It was intended as a time to recognize the prominent role of African Americans in U. S. history.

The story began in 1915, when Woodson founded the Association for the Study of Negro Life and History (ASNLH) which was organized to promote the achievements and accomplishments of black Americans.

Initially, the group recognized a week in February as Negro History Week coinciding with the birthdays of Abraham Lincoln and Frederick Douglas. The first Negro History Week was celebrated in 1926.

By the late 1960's many colleges began celebrating Black History Month in February, and in 1976 President Gerald R. Ford officially proclaimed February as Black History Month, to, "seize the opportunity to honor the too often neglected accomplishments of black Americans in every area of endeavor throughout our history."

Now you know exactly where this is going, or at least you should by now.

It's not so much that I mind there is a Black History Month, but that there is no corresponding White History Month, and me or whoever else would attempt to propose one would be run out of town on the next train, accused of being racist.

So answer me, why can there be so much devoted to the celebration of Black History Month, but not a thought of having a designated month to celebrate the history and achievement of white Americans?

Gosh it sounds racist even to say it.

CNN, the network you have already read a lot about in here, dedicates a huge part of their programming during February to Black History Month.

Reporter Soledad O'Brien started and reports a lengthy segment called 'Black in America' chronicling the stories of blacks and their accomplishments, including the plight of blacks, or where, in her viewpoint, blacks are still being persecuted.

Now, it's not so much that there are such stories, just that you will never see such programs about whites.

Some of the headlines and coverage read: Obama says Black America is Better Off Now, Blogger says America Isn't for Black People, Being Black and Ambiguous in America, and Raising Black Children in America.

There are countless black festivals and 'cultural' festivals and celebrations held all across the country, many in conjunction with Black History Month.

Examples include all sorts of Black Film Festivals (see another chapter herein on the Image Awards and other Black film things).

Other examples of black or 'cultural' celebrations (and the list is far too long to name them all) include the Juneteenth Ohio Festival, the Congo Square Festival in New Orleans, the Satchmo Summerfest, also in the Crescent City, the Afro Dream Fest and the Afro Dream Fest Live Concert, the Fetival Sundiata in Seattle, and the Vision Festival in Brooklynn, just to name a few.

Can you imagine the uproar if someone proposed just one "White Festival?"

The NAACP and every black group imaginable would be tearing up the airwaves and calling for organizers of such an event to be placed on every 'hate' group list out there.

The National Education Association, one of the largest teachers' groups in America, on its website even includes a page about offering specific curriculum to schools, by grade, to help integrate Black History Month into the classroom.

Yet the wonderful book Tom Sawyer, by Mark Twain, an excellent story about boyhood, is still kept out of the classroom for Twain's use of the word, "nigger" throughout its pages.

Postage stamps have commemorated Black History Month.

And products, you name it.

Printables, tons of sites online to purchase the same, t-shirts, calendars, countless books of activities for kids. One online site offers over 23 million items for sale to celebrate Black History Month.

There are even poems, songs and books of famous quotes celebrating Black History Month.

America cannot seem to get enough of Black History Month, or so it seems as the pandering continues to grow in its vibrance.

But dare we ever consider celebrating a White History Month, recognizing white pride and accomplishments?

CNN ran a story on "CNN Tonight" on January 7, 2015, which I feel absolutely proves the lengths to which society has gone in this politically-correct mindset of reverse discrimination as it relates to the idea of one race promoting itself (such as Black History Month) and another race (whites) attempting to.

The story concerned a billboard that had been put up in Harrison, Arkansas, which as many know and as CNN seems to constantly remind us, is the apparent 'home' of the Ku Klux Klan, at least to the extent that one of its highest ranking directors resides there and that the Klan maintains their mailing address there.

The Billboard shows a little white girl with a slogan that reads, "It's NOT Racist to Love Your People." A heart symbol is used to signify the word 'love.'

The billboard contained a website which obviously was promoting the billboard, of www.whiteprideradio.com.

Here is a photograph I took of the billboard on February, 6, 2015:

In the CNN story, Don Lemon was interviewing Thomas Robb, the director of the Knights Club of the Ku Klux Klan and former mayor of Harrison, and was doing everything in his power to accuse the sign of being racist and trying to get Robb to admit it.

Lemon asked Robb why he saw a need for the billboard. Robb responded, "Because white people have the right to love their heritage, to love their culture, to love their people," He didn't add, though I wish he had added, "Gosh if the blacks

Black Pandering

can have a whole month to celebrate their culture with a story every night about it on CNN, then why can't whites have one billboard?"

You see, that is just the point.

The blacks do have their month, and all of the hoopla surrounding their Black History Month.

Whites have none of that, yet are accused of being racist for the placement of one billboard promoting white heritage.

One of the biggest double standards of society, wouldn't you say?

Even Robb, in one of his answers to Lemon in the CNN story, captured in words exactly what I am trying to say, "I think black people should love their heritage (and we all see how society trips all over itself to allow black people to do just that) I think people that are Asian should love their people, I think people that are Mexican should love their people, their culture, I have no problem with that. My problem is the hypocrisy that encourages other races to love their people, but wants to demonize and throw mud at a white person who simply says love your people."

Exactly.

I couldn't have said it better myself!

Now, when talking about heritage and cultural pride, you have to include a discussion about the Confederate flag. (see another chapter devoted to that topic herein)

As you probably do not realize, and it's explained in detail in another chapter herein, the Confederate flag of today was never officially the flag of the Confederate States of America. Further, if you know any history at all, you realize that slavery was NOT the cause of the Civil War. The issue of State's rights was.

Charles G. Ankrom

In fact, and read your history on this, President Lincoln initially never intended to end slavery, just to limit it to the states which had slavery at that time and prevent it from spreading into the new territories that would become states.

As such, Southerners began fighting the Civil War over states' rights and flew their flags, most of which were similar to the Confederate flag as we know it today, in support of state's rights. Their Southern heritage, if you will.

It wasn't until the Emancipation Proclamation of 1863, {which, by the way, ONLY freed the slaves of the Southern states, not the slaves of Northern ones}, that slavery became an issue of the Civil War.

Then the 13th Amendment's passage confirmed the abolition of slavery as a major OUTCOME of the war.

So for whites, and particularly Southern whites, the Confederate flag is clearly a symbol of cultural pride and Southern heritage and should be viewed as such by society, right alongside African Americans celebrating their history and culture through Black History Month.

At least that's the way it should be, if society were truly 'equal' in things related to race.

But we all know society isn't 'equal' when it comes to race, because society allows the pandering of blacks pursuant to and consistent with the politically-correct mindset of reverse discrimination.

And everything about Black History Month, and Black heritage sites, and Black festivals etc. is allowed, praised and encouraged by the media. Let's celebrate Black History. That's great!

But don't you dare get caught flying a Confederate flag.

And never, ever, let us catch you putting up just one billboard in Harrison, Arkansas!

Chapter 10: The Congressional Black Caucus

In no other area are blacks pandered to as much as in politics, and no less than the highest levels of our nation's government, through an organization called the Congressional Black Caucus.

The Congressional Black Caucus is an organization representing black members of the United States Congress.

Membership is exclusive to African Americans.

Exclusive.

If you ask me, that's about as racist as racist can be.

And it's happening openly and obviously at the very top of our nation's government.

Originally called the, "Democratic Select Committee," the group was formed in 1969 by a group of black members of the House of Representatives, including Shirley Chisholm of New York, Louis Stokes of Ohio, and William L. Clay of Missouri.

The group was renamed the Congressional Black Caucus in 1971.

The Caucus formally requests a meeting with the President each year, and is sometimes formally invited to meet the President at the White House.

And I am sure the purpose is to discuss BLACK issues, or issues that affect blacks.

The Congressional Black Caucus, in case you didn't know, has a website.

Look it up.

On the day I am writing this, January 28, 2015, just below the header for the group's website and is a box that reads, "12/03/14 The Congressional Black Caucus members and lawmakers representing New York City said they want an investigation following a grand jury decision not to indict an NYPD officer who was recorded on video putting suspect (Eric Garner) in a chokehold, killing him."

You can go back and pull up headlines from previous months.

This from August, 2014, "CBC members speak on the situation in Ferguson, Missouri." "CBC chair Marsha L. Fudge and ranking member John Conyers Statement on Ferguson, Missouri." Then "Reps Conyers, Clay, and Fudge call on Department of Justice to investigate the death of Michael Brown" This last headline was followed by an opening to a paragraph which read, "Following the tragic killing of Michael Brown, an unarmed African American teenager.....(blah, blah blah)."

I guess what I am trying to point out is that here is an absolutely and totally racial group, by definition, that society and our govenment allows to have a huge and highly placed platform (the U.S. Congress) from which to spew their totally one-sided racially charged ideas.

There is no Congressional White Caucus, with a webpage, that limits membership to whites only, (can you say KKK?) that has a yearly meeting with the President at the White House to discuss WHITE issues.

There is no webpage for such a group with headlines that read such things as, "Further investigation at Ferguson reveals Michael Brown grabbed officer Wilson's gun and attacked him" "Officer Wilson is praised by fellow officers for taking a felony-committing thug off the streeets."

Or how about, "Blacks prove their true 'thug' character by violence after Ferguson." ""Burn this bitch down" statement nets Michael Brown's father Louis Head a 'hate' crime charge."

It sounds silly and racist to even imagine a White Congressional Caucus.

So why do we have a Black one?

And boy DO we have one!

An article in the New York Times on February 10, 2013, written by Eric Lipton and Eric Lightblau, described how the Congressional Black Caucus has become one of the money raising juggernauts in Washington, D.C., and was able to pull in donations from major corporate sponsors because of its having, in addition to its traditional political fundraising arm, which is subject to federal rules, a network of non-regulated, non-profit groups and charities which can take in unlimited funds.

In fact, from 2004-2008 the group's political and charitable branches took in $55 million in corporate and union contributions.

The group's signature legislative dinner and conference is one of the highlights of the Washington, D. C. social life.

The event in 2009 included roof top parties, and a final night black-tie dinner which included President Obama, actor Danny Glover, and musician Wyclef Jean.

The event is lavish to say the least.

Maybe too lavish?

The Southern Company, a major utility company for several southeastern states shelled out $300,000 to host a party at the 2009 event honoring Rep. Barbara Lee of California, the chairwoman of the group. The limousine bill, alone, for the night was $11,000.

The cost for the catering, yes catering, for just one night's event in 2008 was $700,000, which, according to federal records, is more than the group gave out in scholarships for all of 2008.

And then there's this little ditty.

Look up the Congressional Black Caucus on Wikipedia. Scroll down to a paragraph on 'Funding.'

Apparently, prior to 1994, the Congressional Black Caucus actually RECEIVED federal funding as a 'legislative service organization.' I tried and tried to find out if that is still true but had no luck in my research.

It would be absolutely appalling if it were, considering the Times article on all of the money they receive nowadays, and their lavish spending habits.

Ralph Nader once got into a shouting match with the Congressional Black Caucus at a meeting he was attending during his presidential candidacy of 2004.

Apparently the group was urging Nader to give up his presidential bid, due to it hurting the chances of Democratic Presidential nominee John Kerry.

Nader accused Rep Melvin Watt, D-N.C. of uttering an 'obscene racial epithet' at Nader by saying, "You're just another arrogant white man—telling us what we can do—it's all about your ego—another fucking arrogant white man."

Nader wrote to the Caucus and asked for at least an apology, "…. therefore, just as African Americans demanded an apology from Agriculture Secretary Earl Butz and Senator Trent Lott—prior to their resignations and demotions respectively—for their racist comments, I expect that you and the others in the Caucus will exert your moral persuasion and request an apology from Congressman Watt…"

Watt never apologized.

There was also an attempt made by a white congressman to join the all black group.

Black Pandering

In 2006, white candidate Steve Cohen was running for a seat in a Tennessee district that was 60% black. He made a pledge to apply for membership in the group if he won so that he could better represent his constituents.

He did win and did apply.

But his application was denied.

Now the bylaws of the Congressional Black Caucus do not limit membership exclusively to blacks. But former and current members agreed that membership of the caucus should remain, "exclusively black."

Representative William Lacy Clay, Jr. of Missouri, and a son of caucus founder William Lacy Clay, Sr., said, "Mr Cohen asked for admission and he got his answer. He's white and the caucus is black. It's time to move on. We have racial policies to pursue and we are pursuing them, As Mr. Cohen has learned. It's an unwritten rule. It's understood."

In addition Clay also issued the following statement, "Quite simply, Rep. Cohen will have to accept what the rest of the country will have to accept—there has been an unofficial Congressional White Caucus for over 200 years, and now it's our turn to say who can join, 'the club.' He does not and cannot meet the criteria, unless he can change his skin color. Primarily we are concerned with the needs and concerns of the black population, and we will not allow white America to infringe on those objectives."

Now how in the world is that not a "You can't vote because of the color of your skin" or "You are only 3/5ths of a person" or "we serve white people only" type of statement, meaning about as racial of a statement as anyone could ever make?

And goodness gracious, how come America didn't hear anything about it at the time?

I don't recall a single story about that statement in any newspaper, or on CNN, CBS, ABC, NBC, or even Fox, for that matter, not to mention the news sources on the internet.

Yet here was a guy at the top level of our government, a member of the United States House of Representatives no less, one of the most powerful men in this country, making the most racial statement imaginable, telling whites to, "go to the back of the bus," so to speak, all in support of one of the most racial groups in existence by its nature, and none of us heard anything about it?

How in the world could that happen?

Black pandering perhaps?

Blacks can say and do anything they want and society allows them to do so in accordance with this ingrained mindset of reverse discrimination, and excessive black pandering.

Imagine my White Congressional Caucus for a moment. A black congressman has applied for membership in the all-white group.

And a leading white Representative comes out saying something along the same line, "Mr. so and so applied and he got his answer. He's black and the caucus is white. We have RACIAL policies to pursue and we are pursuing them. It's an unwritten rule, it's understood."

And then further, "Mr. so and so will have to accept what the rest of the country will have to accept. We are primarily concerned with the needs and concerns of the WHITE population, and we will not allow black America to infringe on those objectives."

I wrote it out because it sounds absolutely and ridiculously racist when reading it from that perspective.

But the sad point, is that because of our politically-correct mindset of reverse discrimination, blacks can say that 'crap' (excuse me for using such a crude word, but I guess it could have been worse!) but society would never put up with it coming from whites.

Representative Tom Tancredo, R-CO, shortly after Clay's statements, responded with the idea I am trying to get at, in calling for the ending of the Congressional Black Caucus and also the Democratic Congressional Hispanic Caucus, and the Republican Congressional Hispanic Caucus, "It is utterly hypocritical for Congress to extol the virtues of a color-blind society while officially sanctioning caucuses that are based solely on race. If we are serious about achieving the goal of a colorblind society, Congress should lead by example and end these divisive, race-based caucuses."

Amen brother!

Chapter 11: Affirmative Action

Affirmative action is governmental and institutionally-imposed reverse discrimination. Period. Plain and simple. There's just no other way to look at it.

And one need only look at the way affirmative action is DEFINED by our society for proof positive, yes, that's actual PROOF of the existence of my politically-correct mindset of reverse discrimination.

Read the following definitions for affirmative action. Then let's talk!

Yahoo Dictionary defines affirmative action as: A policy or a program that seeks to redress past discrimination through active measures to ensure equal opportunity, as in education and employment.

USLEGAL.com defines affirmative action as: The process of a business or governmental agency in which it gives special rights of hiring or advancement to ethnic minorities to make up for past discrimination against that minority.

Investopedia online defines affirmative action as: A policy in which an individual's color, race, religion or national origin are taken into account by a business or government in order to increase the opportunities provided to an underrepresented part of society.... It is often considered a means of countering historical discrimination against a particular group.

Wikipedia defines affirmative action as: The policy of favoring members of a disadvantaged group who are perceived to suffer from discrimination within a culture.

The Free Dictionary Thesaurus defines affirmative action as: A policy designed to redress past discrimination against women and minority groups through measures to improve their economic and educational opportunities."

And then there's good old Webster, or Merriam-Webster as the case may be, who defines affirmative action as: The practice of improving the educational and job opportunities of members of groups that have not been treated fairly in the past because of their race, sex, etc.

Now, it's not so much the words used in the various definitions of affirmative action above that prove the existence of my politically-correct mindset of reverse discrimination, for the definitions all seem to say about the same thing.

Rather, it's the words that are MISSING from all of the above definitions which serve as absolute PROOF of the mindset of which I speak.

I come to this conclusion not by mere happenstance, but from a general notion that these companies and organizations, in crafting common definitions for the public to use, would attempt to use all of the facts that are consistently and regularly present about a particular word they are attempting to define.

But in the case of affirmative action they seem to have left out one half of the entire equation. For in every case of affirmative action, something else exists which is addressed with the addition of those words I deem to be MISSING.

Those words are, "at the expense of, or detriment to, another group."

Go back now and read the definitions above but add those missing words to the end of each definition and see if you don't agree that the missing words makes the definitions more complete as to the real definition of affirmative action, at least according to how affirmative action plays out in society.

You know and I know that in every single case where, "a program... to redress past discrimination" was put in place, or where "opportunities.. were... increased.... to counter historical discrimination," or where "special rights' were given to minorities, that it was always, always, only accomplished, "at the expense of, or detriment to another group," and probably whites. For more often than not, it consisted of a black person getting a job or a school admission spot, "at the expense of, or detriment to..." a white person.

It's this blatant and inexcusable omission of those 'missing' words from those definitions for affirmative action by some very reputable companies and organizations which I contend is absolute PROOF of the existence of a politically-correct mindset of reverse discrimination.

For this mindset causes society to pander to the black community, and tilt those definitions heavily to the discrimination side of the story and is so ingrained, that the definition makers have drafted the definitions accordingly.

Gosh, in reading those definitions I am surprised that none of them just went ahead and threw the word 'slavery' into the mix. Read some of those definitions again, "... historical discrimination..." "... past discrimination..." "... discrimination within a culture..." "... a means of countering historical discrimination against a group."

Just say it, you know you want to—slavery!

Affirmative action is getting back at whites for slavery!

The concept of affirmative action is not new. The term was first used by President John F. Kennedy in 1961 in an executive order to promote actions that achieved non-discrimination.

Then came the Civil Rights Act of 1964, which prohibited discrimination of all kinds because of race, religion, color, and nationality.

The first enforcement was from President Johnson in 1965, again by an executive order which required government contractors to "take affirmative action" toward prospective minority employees in all aspects of hiring and employment.

Quota is a word that goes hand in hand, and is almost synonymous with affirmative action. Educational Institutions began to use quotas, or specific numbers, usually percentages, in the selection of minority students for admission. Companies and corporations then followed suit as to hiring practices.

These quotas, put in place through Affirmative Action Plans, or APA's, became very popular, the norm the fact, during the late 1960's and 1970's as a way for colleges and employers to attempt to be in compliance with the federal law.

As you can imagine, many more-qualified students, usually white ones, were denied admission to schools, or jobs due to the existence of these quotas.

Talk about pandering to blacks!

Then in 1978 came the landmark decision in the University of California v Bakke. Allan Bakke was a white applicant who was denied admission twice to the University of California, Davis, Medical School, even though his scores were higher than some of the minority students who were admitted.

The University of California, Davis, Medical School had a policy, or quota, of accepting 16 minority students out of every 100 students. Bakke alleged his being denied admission was a violation of the Equal Protection Clause of the Fourteenth Amendment of the United States Constitution. And guess what?

He won!

The United States Supreme Court ruled that while race was a legitimate factor in school admissions, the use of such inflexible quotas the medical school had set aside was not. Thus, the Supreme Court imposed limitations on affirmative action to insure that providing greater opportunities for minorities did not come "at the expense of" the rights of the majority.

Note the use by the Supreme Court, way back in 1978, of those words I allege are missing from the definitions of affirmative action at the beginning of this chapter—"at the expense of."

In even simpler terms, the Supreme Court was saying that affirmative action was unfair if it led to reverse discrimination.

However, the next important decision concerning affirmative action came in 1980 and muddied up the pot again. While Bakke had struck down strict quotas, the Supreme Court in Fullilove v Klutznick ruled that modest quotas were perfectly constitutional.

In Fullilove, the Supreme Court upheld a federal law requiring that 15 percent of federal funds for public works be set aside for minority contractors.

Several years went by with only a few cases that touched on affirmative action, but nothing major.

That is, until 2003 when the next big decision on the subject came out, where the Supreme court upheld the University of Michigan Law School's policy that race can be one of many factors considered by colleges when selecting their students because it furthers, "a compelling interest in obtaining the educational benefits that flow from a diverse student body."

Then in the summer of 2013, the Supreme Court ruled in Fisher v. The University of Texas, in what seems to be the current state of the law on affirmative action, that universities can continue using race as a factor in admissions to achieve diversity, but only when they prove, "that available, workable, race-neutral alternatives do not suffice."

So, what's it all mean? Who really knows?

To the average Joe, affirmative action was legal, then not, then legal again, then kinda legal, then still kinda legal but less legal, etc.

I have to wonder what approach educational institutions and employers have been using during these flip-flop years as they struggled to figure out what to do in the admissions and hiring process.

I can guess. It was probably better to be safe than sorry, or as us rednecks would put it, "cover your ass."

And because of that approach, try to imagine how many blacks were given "special rights" in obtaining a spot in a college or graduate school class, or given "favorable" treatment "as a member of a disadvantaged group" in being given a job in place of, or "at the expense of" whites, who in many of those instances, if not all of them, were more qualified.

As such, affirmative action is simply, without any doubt, governmental or institutionally- imposed reverse discrimination, or reverse discrimination by law!

Or at least it is by the definition that it should have, and which by the way, myself, along with the United State Supreme Court happen to give it.

Further and perhaps more importantly, the way in which it is NOT defined is absolute proof of the existence of my politically-correct mindset of reverse discrimination.

Pandering to the supreme!

Chapter 12: African American Museums

Have you ever visited an African America museum? Or how about America's Black Holocaust Museum, which likens the plight of the Africa Americans slaves to the Nazi Holocaust of World War II?

I bet you didn't know that there was an Association of African American Museums. Or that many of the African American Museums get some of their funding from the federal government, though most comes from state or local municipal funding.

There are about 85 major African American Museums located in the country, not to mention numerous smaller ones and then places which are called African American Heritage sites.

I wonder how many White American Museums get funding from the federal government. Shoot, I wonder whether a White American Museum even exists. I couldn't find one.

Now most blacks and some whites will, and have argued that every mainline museum is a white museum. Nina Simon, who is executive director of the Santa Cruz Museum of Art and History, who is white, asserted in an article on Museums 2.0 blog page that, "The vast majority of American Museums are institutions of white privilege. They tell histories of white male conquest...... The popular reference point for what a museum is—a temple for contemplation-- is based on a Euro-centric set of myths and implies white behavior."

White male conquest?

Really?

I toured the World War II museum in New Orleans the other day and it contained one entire section and many other exhibits geared specifically toward the role of blacks in WWII, including the history of segregation of the military during the war. Blacks were grouped in units together and most of them had assignments other than combat. But some exhibits highlighted military units made up of all blacks, toward the later part of the war, which did get into actual combat and performed quite admirably, most notably the Tuskegee Flying Tigers.

One tidbit I found interesting was that in the military hospitals during WWII blood was even segregated, meaning whites could not receive black blood and vice versa.

In addition, I have also been to other museums around the country and most do have exhibits on blacks and black history. So I dare say that Ms. Simon is way off base.

She further asserted in her article that, "They (museums) present masterpieces by white male artists and innovations by white male scientists…. The White privilege frame distorts the extent to which museums can represent and reflect the diversity of humanity….."

I wonder if Ms. Simon even considered that the reason the mainline museums highlight white masterpieces and white innovations is that whites were simply more talented, artistic, and creative, than blacks at previous times in history? Could it be the artwork and innovations of the whites were just better than the artwork and innovations of blacks?

Now some may think that sounds racist but that is exactly the explanation given by blacks and society when whites dare question the disproportionate number (compared to population percentages) of blacks in the NBA.

Whites are never allowed by society to claim discrimination in basketball because blacks are just better basketball players. "White Men Can't Jump." Remember?

But lest I digress, this is just another area where blacks are pandered to.

The first African American Museum was located Hampton, Virginia in 1868. And prior to 1950 there were about 30 African American Museums, most of which were located at historically black colleges and universities. (see the chapter herein on those things)

By 1991 there were as many as 150 African American Museums located in 37 states. The largest one to date is the Charles H. Wright Museum of African American History, in Detroit, Michigan which contains over 135,000 square feet of exhibits. It will, however, be dwarfed in size by the Smithsonian Institution's National Museum of African American History and Culture, which is due to be completed in 2016. When finished it will encompass 350,000 square feet and 10 stories, 5 underground and 5 above. It is estimated to cost $250 million.

The Smithsonian's National Museum of African American History and Culture already has a website. The website claims that the museum, "will be a place where all Americans can learn about the richness and diversity of the African American experience, what it means to their lives, and how it helped us shape this nation." The mission statement of the museum explains further, "This museum seeks to help all Americans remember, and by remembering, this institution will stimulate dialogue about race and help to foster a spirit of reconciliation and healing."

The National Museum of African American History and Culture DID receive federal support.

That's right, our government panders to blacks by financially supporting the National Museum of African American History and Culture.

The government allowed the museum to be placed on the Washington Monument grounds (free land?) and in 2003, Congress appropriated $17 million for the planning of the museum and another $15 million for "educational programs."

These programs includes grants for African American Museums to help them improve their operations and collections, grants to African American Museums for internships and fellowships, scholarships for individuals pursuing careers in African American studies, grants to promote the modern day study of slavery throughout the world, and grants to help African American Museums to build their endowments.

The front design of the museum will include a pond, garden and bridge so that visitors will have to, "cross over the water"—just like slaves did when they came to America.

So here we have had our highest levels of government (Congress and the President) taking up the cause of a museum dedicated solely to African American history and providing some of the financing.

Now I am no so upset with that idea in and of itself. But when paired with my notion of a politically-correct mindset of reverse discrimination that keeps Congress and the President from EVER supporting the same for a museum dedicated solely to whites, then it becomes atrocious.

Don't you agree?

Interesting to note is a portion of a statement by Era L Marshall, the director of the Office of Equal Employment and Minority Affairs, concerning businesses or organizations that do business with the Smithsonian' that the institution, "... strongly adheres to a policy of equal opportunity in ALL aspects of our business relationships."

Did she say ALL?

I wonder how far I would get if I went to the Smithsonian to propose a "business relationship' for the construction of a National Museum of White American History and Culture?

You know the answer and I do too!

But seriously, if they are building a museum dedicated solely to black history doesn't "equal opportunity" mean that there should be one dedicated solely to white history as well?

Or has the pandering to blacks reached the stage where such a thought is never to be considered?

What do you think?

USA Today online ran a story on February 14, 2014 highlighting the "Ten Best Places Where Black History Comes Alive." The article was glowing in its praise and quoted Robert Luckett, an assistant professor and director of the Margaret Walker Center at Jackson State University in Jackson, Mississippi, who said, "Museums give us an opportunity to reflect that African American history is American history."

Doesn't he really mean that African American history is A PART of American history?

The Association of African American Museums is an organization whose mission is, "to support African and African American focus museums nationally and internationally."

The association has a website. Look it up. I was shocked, though perhaps I shouldn't have been, to see that a significant part of the website is dedicated to information and help on how its member museums can get grants.

That's right, federal funding.

Federal funding is apparently available from the federal government through the American Alliance of Museums Connect program through the U.S. Department of State's Bureau of Educational and Cultural Affairs.

Federal funding for a group that also included on its website this statement from Sam Black, the association's president on November 28, 2014, "The Association of African American Museums supports the families of Michael Brown, Trayvon Martin, Jordan Miles, Jonny Gammage, and many others who are examples of how racism gives birth to injustice. As a national organization and like most Americans of conscience we cannot sit idly by as unchecked police power cheapens our lives and creates a, "failure of government not seen since the dark days of lynching."

Uh, wait a second Mr Black.

You CAN sit idly by, and probably should be sitting idly by, and not involving yourself in politics if you receive any sort of federal funds (read that as my tax dollars and the tax dollars of millions of other white people) whatsoever.

Further as to funding for African American Museums, Randall A. Williams and Michael Worth of George Washington University, were quoted in an article by Rick Cohen printed in the Non Profit Quarterly's February 1, 2015 edition, which concerned the woeful financial state of many African American Museums, including the Wright. They suggested that African American Museums are underfunded due to, "historical barriers (and) cultural preferences in charitable giving...." This caused Cohen to further question in his article, "Are African American Museums simply troubled because of what they are and represent?"

To that I say simply—give me a break. You have the audacity to imply that African American Museums in this country, of which there are many, and which there are some that receive federal funding, are being discriminated against?

I challenge Mr. Cohen to tell me how many White American Museums there are and whether they are funded by the federal government. He can't.

As for America's Black Holocaust Museum, there is one, or kinda. I guess a physical brick and mortar building for this museum did previously exist. Now this 'museum' is virtual, which is a fancy way of saying it's on the internet, or online.

The mission of this virtual museum is, "to educate the public about the ongoing injustices endured by people of African American heritage….. and to provide visitors with opportunities to rethink their assumptions about race and racism."

Well I'm sorry but I don' think I need to rethink my assumptions about racism.

Their website, I mean America's Black Holocaust virtual Museum attempts to call the 400 year history of slavery the "Black Holocaust" and equate it with the Nazi Holocaust of 1941-1945 and the systematic mass murder of millions of European Jews during those years of World War II.

Not even close, by my way of thinking. I don't recall having seen trainloads of blacks marched into gas chambers to be extinguished.

One of the 'reasons' set forth for the continued existence of a "Black Holocaust," among others, is that the net worth of white families is 22 times the net worth of black families, and that since the 1970's the unemployment rate for blacks is double the national average. Now I agree there are problems of black poverty and black unemployment that society needs to address. But these hardly constitute a "Black Holocaust."

Thus, the existence of all of these African American Museums and the Association of African American Museums which leads the charge for federal funding, along with numerous African American Heritage sites, and the fact that the Smithsonian, the most respected museum of all, is even building an African American Museum, together with the total absence of any White American Museums, is just another area where blacks are being pandered to, and the politically-correct mindset of reverse discrimination is strongly rearing its ugly head.

And you can imagine, like myself, that this is not about to change anytime soon, if ever at all!

Chapter 13: The Confederate Flag and the Black Power Salute

Symbols of Hate?

We all know of the uproar the use of the Confederate flag causes nowadays. It's a major issue in society. A symbol of hate, it is called. But have you heard anyone complain about the traditional Black Power salute and whether it also is a symbol of hate? You know the answer.

Now, the Black Power salute, a clenched raised fist, did not originate with the Black Panther Party in the 1960's. It's origins as a sign of power and unity go way back beyond that. But according to a Factbox article in 2013, the clenched fist's most wide usage was by the Black Panther Party in the 1960's.

And who can forget watching or seeing later in pictures how American Olympic athletes Tommie Smith and John Carlos gave the Black Power salute on the medal stand at the 1968 Summer Olympics in Mexico City during the playing of the American National Anthem.? That now infamous display got them banned from the Olympics for life, but more importantly ingrained that salute, that image, that defiance onto the minds of millions of Americans, many of which, at least from the silent white majority, associate that image with blacks in general. (also see the chapter herein on 'thug mentality.')

Now I will admit the use of the traditional Black Power salute is perhaps not as prevalent as at earlier times in our history, even though it has made a comeback during recent events associated with the deaths of Trayvon Martin, Michael Brown, Eric Garner, and most recently Freddie Gray in Baltimore. But I have never, ever heard it alleged to be a symbol of hate, even in these most recent events. Have you?

Why not, when you consider how closely it was associated with violence in the protests of blacks against segregation, particularly in the 1960's and

70's? Countless pictorial images consist of members of the Black Panther/Black Power movement with their fists raised, many times accompanied by military dress, and arms, and associated with speeches by members spewing forth threats of violence against whites.

If you are old enough to remember, the civil rights movement of the 1960's had multiple faces. We all know of the peaceful non-violent protests of Dr. Martin Luther King, Jr. and his followers. And his accomplishments seem to be remembered the most, perhaps because of his violent death in 1968.

But not to be left out of history is the Black Panther party and their notions of defeating segregation with whatever actions were necessary, including violence, espousing the ideas of Malcom X who had been assassinated just prior to the party's founding. His ideas were a huge influence on the party.

FBI director J. Edgar Hoover once called the Black Panther party, "the greatest threat to the internal security of the country."

The party reached a peak of its existence in 1970 with several thousand members and offices in 68 American cites.

Were they violent? Here are some of the facts.

From the beginning their militancy came with a reputation for violence. The party was based in California which at that time had on open-carry policy on guns, meaning that party members could openly carry rifles or loaded shotguns as long as they were exhibited publicly and not pointed at anyone. They carried these guns and chanted slogans such as, "The Revolution has come. It's time to pick up the gun. Off the pigs." I'm sure you can imagine how this reinforced their reputation as a violent organization.

In 1967, 27 members of the Black Panther party carried loaded guns into the California State Assembly to protest the consideration of a law which would make it illegal to publicly carry loaded firearms in the state of California. The incident got a lot of national attention and several members of the party were arrested.

Black Pandering

Also in 1967, party leader Huey Newton was charged with murdering Oakland police officer John Frey. He was convicted of manslaughter, but the conviction was later overturned.

In 1968, party member Bobby Hutton was killed and party member Eldridge Cleaver injured in a shootout with Oakland police. Two police officers were also shot. Although Cleaver initially claimed that he and Hutton had been ambushed by the police, he later allegedly admitted to other party members that he had led a Panther group on a deliberate ambush of the police, provoking the shootout.

And who can forget watching or seeing later in pictures how American Olympic athletes Tommie Smith and John Carlos gave the Black Power salute on the medal stand at the 1968 Summer Olympics in Mexico City during the playing of the American National Anthem.? That now infamous display got them banned from the Olympics for life, but more importantly ingrained that salute, that image, that defiance onto the minds of millions of Americans, many of which, at least from the silent white majority, associate that image with blacks in general. (also see the chapter herein on 'thug mentality.')

In 1974, the party's leader Huey Newton was arrested and charged with assaults on police officers. He fled to Cuba, to avoid further prosecution for the murder of 18 year old Kathleen Smith, a prostitute. Although Newton had admitted to friends that Kathleen Smith was his first, "non-political murder" he was acquitted at trial, very probably because one witness' testimony was impeached by her admission that she had used marijuana the night of the murder and by another prostitute witness recanting her testimony.

In 1977, Flores Forbes, the party's assistant chief of staff, led a botched assassination attempt against one of the witnesses who was scheduled to testify in Newton's trial. This fiasco resulted in the deaths of two party members.

Or how about the disappearance of the bookkeeper of the group Betty Van Patter on December 13, 1974. Her severely beaten body was found some time later. And while there was never enough evidence for charges, it was hypothesized that the Black Panther party leadership were responsible.

In fact, some commentators contended the party was more criminal than political, due to the violence and infighting within the party and their involvement in criminal activities.

And with these recent uproars mentioned above, a New Black Panther Party has made its presence known. And if you have been watching any of the media coverage lately, you can see the revival of the Black Power Salute, alongside the new, "Black Lives Matter" and "Hands up Don't Shoot" slogans that have now evolved, from the happenings in Ferguson, New York City, and Baltimore.

The salute, the crimes, and the violence. And recently the violence has reminded the old timers of the race riots of the 1960's. Hand in hand. But never, never anything about the black power salute being a symbol of hate. And why not?

In a world of true equality between the races, if the Confederate flag is to be considered a symbol of hate, then a normal person would also consider the Black Power salute a symbol of hate as well. But alas, our world is not one of true equality between the races as long as there persists this mindset of reverse discrimination so deeply ingrained in our society, and as long as blacks are pandered to the way that they are.

The Confederate flag is probably one of the most inflammatory and controversial icons of the society in which we live.

It is also, perhaps, one of the most misunderstood.

The flag we all know as the Confederate flag, flew over the capital of South Carolina until 2000, when it was taken down, but allowed to be displayed on the capitol grounds on a soldier's monument. South Carolina officials said it was a symbol of "heritage" and "Southern Pride"

Black Pandering

The NCAA, however continues to not allow predetermined sporting championship events to be held in South Carolina because of this. And the NAACP has a boycott of South Carolina as well.

Blacks everywhere see the flag as a symbol of slavery, racism, and hate. Whites and particularly southern whites contend the flag is a symbol of southern culture and pride, a proud emblem of southern heritage.

Confederate flags on license plates is offered in nine states by the Sons of Confederate Veterans, and efforts are underway to make them accepted in other states as well. The NAACP is opposing these efforts.

The Anti-Defamation League, on a website page labeled 'hate on display' has the Confederate flag listed as a "general racist symbol" It's right there alongside the German swastika, and many lesser recognized white supremacist symbols and logos, and of course, the noose. Nowhere on the same page is the Black Power salute. Interesting. Expected, but interesting.

All one needs to do is look back at the history of what has become known as the Confederate flag to realize it was definitely NOT created as a symbol of hate, and was NOT intended to be used then, nor ever intended to be used as such.

Instead, it came to be out of various expressions of state and battle battalion pride. Early history clearly shows it was never used in direct correlation with feelings against slavery.

In fact, the Confederacy went through a number of various flags and designs from several of the Southern States and southern battle groups, and it was from these that the flag referred to as the Confederate flag came into being.

Truth be told, the flag that today we call the Confederate flag NEVER OFFICIALLY represented the Confederate States of America! This is kind of humorous, considering the "greatest racist symbol" status previously referred to. I guess these harsh feelings for the Confederate flag are a product of my politically-correct mindset of reverse discrimination.

A discussion of the Confederate flag must necessarily include something about the Civil War and the true cause of the Civil War and the perpetual question of whether or not the Civil War was a war about slavery.

There are literally hundreds of books, and probably hundreds of classes taught in colleges across the USA dealing with just that question alone. And we do not have the time or space for a complete discussion.

My short answer is that the Civil War was clearly not CAUSED by the slavery issue, although the termination of slavery as an institution was a major OUTCOME of the Civil War.

While President Lincoln clearly made his personal feelings against slavery known, politically early on he was merely opposed to the expansion of slavery, feeling that the federal government was prevented by the Constitution from banning, or doing away with slavery in those state where it already existed.

True. Look it up.

It wasn't until later in the Civil War, and specifically with the Emancipation Proclamation in 1863, (which was a tactic of war as much as a deep desire to free the slaves) and the 13th Amendment to the Constitution in 1865 that slavery became inexplicably linked to the Civil War.

One interesting tidbit is that the Emancipation Proclamation ONLY freed slaves in the Southern states. It did NOT free slaves in any of the Northern states, or those states remaining in the Union.

For the southern states, the Civil War was always about the issue of state's rights versus the power of the federal government. While slavery became an issue, is was not the major issue, just a part.

As such, the flags used by the Confederacy, and the states thereof, were created and used as symbols of state pride and Southern nationalism, and not symbols of pro-slavery, or hate against blacks, not in the least.

So one must ask how could today's Confederate flag, which again, was never the true flag of the Confederate States of America anyway, even be considered a symbol about hate and slavery, which again, was not even the major issue of the Civil War?

If we lived in a world of true equality of the races, and legally we do, you would have to accept the flying of today's Confederate flag as a symbol of such 'Southern' heritage much the same way society allows and recognizes Black History Month as an expression of African American culture and heritage, (see the chapter herein on Black History Month) and in the same way society allows for the Black Power Salute of the past and present to not even remotely be considered as a symbol of hate.

But we don't. Instead, the politically-correct mindset of reverse discrimination doesn't allow a level playing field.

And Black History Month, and black cultural festivals, and black museums, and black this and black that continue to grow in popularity as it's politically-correct to allow them to do so, while it's always considered racist for certain whites to display their symbol of pride, the Confederate flag.

And one similar recent example shows the absurd degree to which the pandering of blacks has been taken.

In March of 2015, the University of Georgia administrators of fraternities and sororities decided to ban the southern traditional 'hoop' skirts from all events over concerns they might look racist.

Victor Wilson, UGA's vice president for student affairs explained that the ban was due to concerns over what "message" the skirt might send, comparing it to a previous ban of Confederate uniforms.

Charles G. Ankrom

Hoop skirts?

Racist?

An ingrained mindset of reverse discrimination?

Make that question rhetorical.

Chapter 14: The BET

Black Entertainment Television, or BET, is a basic cable and satellite television channel which is owned by the BET networks division of Viacom.

Viacom is a massive American global mass media company with interests primarily in cable television and cinema. It is the world's 6th largest media company in terms of revenue, and stands alongside the likes of Disney, Comcast, Time Warner, CBS and Twenty First Century Fox.

One might think that such a large company would be somewhat concerned about owning what looks like, from all appearances, a totally racist company.

But apparently the folks at Viacom have learned, just like myself, and hopefully you, from this book, that the society in which they exist, and from whom they make their money, has long ago bought into pandering to blacks and the politically-correct mindset of reverse discrimination which allows for there to even be a Black Entertainment Television channel in the first place, while never allowing for a corresponding White Entertainment Television channel to exist.

Programming on the network consists of rap, hip hop, and R &B music, original and acquired television series, and movies released via home video. As of August 2013, just over 91 million, yes million, households in America receive BET.

Black Entertainment Television began on January 25, 1980. BET's initial programming was built around Nickelodeon, and it wasn't until 1983 that it became a full-time channel, with a lineup consisting of music videos and reruns of black sitcoms.

BET News was launched in 1988, with anchor Ed Gorden. He later hosted other special programs such as 'Black Men Speak Out: The Aftermath,' which related to the 1992 Los Angeles riots, and others along that line including 'Conversations with Ed Gorden.'

In the 1990's came programming which consisted primarily of black jazz artists, and a joint venture with Starz movie channel to form a premium channel featuring African American-oriented movies called BET Movies.

BET Walk of Fame awards were created in 1995, and BET hosts an annual charitable Walk of Fame ceremony, where of course black entertainers and artists are honored.

Further, the company established the BET Awards in 2001, for the purpose of honoring the accomplishments of African Americans and other minorities in music, sports, acting, and other achievements for each year. These awards are presented annually on BET.

Many scholars and others within the African American community have argued that BET justifies racism and perpetuates it by effecting the stereotypes of African Americans, which affects the psyche of its younger viewers through bombardment of negative images of African Americans.

The channel was criticized in 2006 for not broadcasting live the funeral of Coretta Scott King, choosing instead to honor Mrs. King with special features broadcast throughout the following days. For failing to broadcast the funeral live as most other networks had done, the National Association of Black Journalists gave BET its Thumbs Down Award. (Wait, we have a group called the National Association of Black Journalists?)

In recent years, the channel has come under criticism, and even protest, for presenting negative stereotypes of black people through the broadcasting of more and more of today's videos and the depictions of sexuality, and profane and violent conduct. (See my chapter on "thug mentality" where I discuss this evolution of black rap.. music)

BET co-founder Sheila Johnson was interviewed in 2010 and said that even she was 'ashamed' at what BET had become, adding, "I don't watch it.

I suggest to my kids that they don't watch it," further explaining that "When we started BET, it was going to be the 'Ebony' magazine on television.... but the problem is that then the video revolution started up..... I didn't like the way women were being portrayed in these videos."

The company became the first black-owned business to be listed on the New York Stock exchange in 1991. But it lost its black-owned status when it was bought out by Viacom in 2003, for $3 billion.

In short the storyline for a television channel devoted primarily, if not entirely to blacks was nothing but a tremendous success.

So how about that white television channel? You know the one that ......?

You see, I could not finish that sentence because as we all know, there isn't a television channel devoted entirely to whites. And as we also know, society will never, ever allow such a television channel due to the mindset of reverse discrimination and the excessive pandering to blacks.

Can you imagine a white television channel with a news program daily that gave updates on the progress whites had made, or not, in society for any given day?

Or how about the WET (White Entertainment Television) Awards honoring those white artists who have made contributions in areas similar to the BET Awards.

The more I even mention it, the more racist it looks doesn't it?

Chapter 15: The Image Awards

How about a little black pandering in the entertainment industry?

The Image Wards are awards given by the NAACP to honor outstanding people of color in music, film, television, and literature. They are similar to the Oscars and Emmys.

There are 35 categories of awards which are voted on by members of the NAACP. Honorary awards are also given, including the Chairman's Award, the President's Award, the Entertainer of the Year Award, and an Image Award Hall of Fame.

This year's awards show was the 46th version of the awards and aired live on February 6, 2015 at 8 pm on TV One.

The Image Awards were first given out in 1967, and were first televised in 1994 on the Fox Network. The first live broadcast occurred in 2007 for the 38th edition, and also aired on Fox.

The Image Awards have not been without their share of controversy. Some critics have previously complained that certain nominees were undeserving of honor, most usually because of pending serious criminal charges which critics argued overshadowed the nominees artistic achievements. Examples include Tupac Shakur, who was nomination for Outstanding Actor in a Movie, "Poetic Justice," in 1994, after being charged with sexual assault in 1993. And in 2004, R. Kelly's "Chocolate Factory" was nominated for Outstanding Album while he was under indictment for child pornography.

Nominee Cedric the Entertainer was nominated for Outstanding Supporting Actor for his role in "Barbershop," which was also nominated for Outstanding Motion Picture in 2003, but he and the movie were criticized for the portrayals of civil rights figures. In the movie, Cedric makes questionable comments about Dr. Martin Luther King, Jr., Rosa Parks, Jesse Jackson, and Michael Jackson. The controversy resulted in Rosa Parks boycotting the awards.

Past winners of the Outstanding Motion Picture have included such recognizable names as "Ray," "Precious," "The Help," "The Color Purple," and last year's winner, which also won Best Picture at the Academy Awards, "12 Years a Slave." This year's winner was "Selma" about the civil rights march of Dr. Martin Luther King, Jr. across the Edmund Pettis bridge in Selma, Alabama, in the 1960's.

Outstanding Actresses have included the likes of—Whoopi Goldberg, Angela Bassett, Viola Davis, and Halle Berry.

Outstanding Actors have included—Denzel Washington, Morgan Freeman, Forest Whitaker, and Danny Glover.

If you read the list of nominees you might wonder how some white folks get on that list. Take Sandra Bullock for instance, who was nominated for Outstanding Actress in 2009, for "The Blind Side." Bullock won the Academy Award for Best Actress for "The Blind Side."

Apparently, the NAACP has expanded the award to include and recognize, "the accomplishments of those individuals who have worked for positive social change within the industry and the community," according to NAACP spokesman John C.. White.

In other words, or I guess in my words, awards can be given to whites who have championed the cause of blacks. (I dare not say what the KKK would call these people)

Now if the existence of the NAACP's Image Awards isn't enough for you, there is also the African American Film Critics Association. This association was formed in 2003 and consists of a group of African American film critics who also give out various awards for excellence at the end of each year.

Part of the mission of the AAFCA is to produce awareness for films with widespread appeal for members of the black community, while stressing the importance of films which are produced, written, directed and starring people of African American descent.

The AAFCA also gives out awards for categories similar to the Image Awards and does present an award for Special Achievement, which has been won by the likes of Spike Lee and Jamie Foxx.

Membership in the AAFCA is geographically diverse, and diverse across various media, including radio, television, online, and print. All members, however, are black.

The group also sponsors special programs such as a panel discussion about the concept of diversity in modern film. The panel explores the role cinema plays to go beyond a simplistic message of tolerance.

Another program offered is the Junior Critic Program, which works with historically black colleges and universities to select four journalism students to cover a film promotional event as a journalist.

A huge scandal rocked the AAFCA in 2009. The big winner that year was "Precious: Based on the novel 'Push' by Sapphire" The movie won best picture, best director, best screenplay, and best supporting actress. However, the film's main star Gabourey Sidibe, did NOT win for best actress. That award went to Nicole Beharie of "American Violet," It was later reported by Roger Friedman of 'The Hollywood Reporter' that the tally had been manipulated by the AAFCA president Gil Robertson IV, who was to receive a bribe in the form of a donation from the producers affiliated with "American Violet."

Now if this isn't enough award groups dedicated to black films and black actors and black actresses, there are also the awards given out by the Black Film Critics Association.

As for festivals which are dedicated to black films, and black actors and black actresses there are the Toronto Black Film Festival, the Philadelphia Black Film Festival, the Miami Black Film Festival, the San Diego Black Film Festival, the San Francisco Black Film Festival, the Black Harvest International Festival of Film in Chicago, the Cascade Festival of Films in Portland, Oregon, the New York African Film Festival, the Hollywood Black Film Festival, the American Black Film Festival, the BlackStar Film Festival, the National Black Theatre Festival, the Pan African Film and Arts in Los Angeles, the New York African Diaspora, an also something called the Urban Film Series. And who would want to forget the Urbanworld Black Film Festival?

There's even a top 12 Black Film Festivals list on "The Film Reporter" located on the web, not to be outdone, of course, by the Top 10 Black Film Festivals list on "Rollingout," also online. There is even a Black Filmmaker Magazine.

I guess the blacks are just not content for their film achievements to be considered only by the Academy Awards, Golden Globes, and the other generic, all-races included awards shows.

I sure can't imagine why the blacks wouldn't be willing to cast their lot into letting the Academy Awards, Golden Globes and the other generic, all-races included awards shows, being their only places for competition, considering the pandering that blacks receive in today's society due to my politically-correct mindset of reverse discrimination.

"Twelve Years a Slave" was a big winner last year in the Oscars. Halle Berry has won an Oscar. Sidney Poitier? Didn't he win as well? And each year it seems there are sufficient numbers of blacks and black films nominated for these awards. The exception is "Selma" for 2015 and I discuss my views as to why it might have been left out of the Oscar party this year, except for its 'best movie' nomination, which I discuss in another chapter herein.

I have presented all of these facts so you can get a scope of the popularity (the extent of the black pandering) of all of these awards and festivals dedicated solely to black films and black actors and black actresses. These have not only existed, but have grown in scope and number and been allowed to flourish tremendously in our society.

And they have so flourished without there ever being any cries of racism about their existence.

None.

I mean, really? A film award show for black films only? How is that not racist?

It's obvious the whites do NOT have their separate White Image Awards presented by a group called the National Association for the Advancement of White People.

And it's just as obvious there never will be such awards for whites. Not in a million years!

As you can see, the politically-correct mindset of reverse discrimination is alive and well in Hollywood!

And considering this year's Image Awards were the 46th version of the same, it's safe to say that none of that's about to change anytime soon.

Chapter 16: If "Blackish," Then "Whiteish?"

In the fall of 2014, it appears the blacks and society, along with NBC, bolstered by my notion of a politically-correct mindset of reverse discrimination decided to just throw it in the face of whites everywhere with the new sitcom, "Blackish."

Black pandering to the maximum degree if you ask me.

I for one, was appalled, How could NBC put such a racist titled show on the air. And where was "Whiteish?"

You and I, and society, knows that there will never be a show called "Whiteish." Not until the cows come home would that ever happen.

But here it was-- "Blackish."

The show had approximately 11 million viewers in its debut, and has managed to keep most of them.

The show is styled similar to "The Cosby Show" of the 1980's and 90's, which became one of the most popular television shows in history. And even though the playing out of the racial themes is subtle, much like "The Cosby Show," it comes right into the homes and down the throats of a mostly white America with that title that isn't the least bit subtle -- "Blackish."

It's not a subtle title like "The Cosby Show" gave us, or even one like "The Jeffersons," but as racist a title as could ever be found, when you consider there is and never will be a "Whiteish" sitcom, or a "Black Men Can't Read" movie for that matter.

The sitcom is about an upwardly mobile black family living is suburban Los Angeles. The father of this family, played by Anthony Anderson, is a black advertising executive from a working class background.

Charles G. Ankrom

The storyline is how the family has moved into a middle class, mostly white, neighborhood, and the father is worried that his children are losing touch with their African American heritage. For example his son wants to play hockey instead of basketball.

Talk about playing right into black stereotypes!

I think I remember one episode where the daughter was selling lemonade on the street. The black mother, who happens to be a doctor in the storyline, played by Tracee Ellis-Ross, was encouraging and admiring the child's entrepreneurial spirit when a middle class white neighbor lady comes by. The neighbor assumes that the black family needs money (if they have resorted to having to have the daughter sell lemonade on the street) and even offers help. The black mother, again a doctor, is embarrassed that whites are once again making stereotypical assumptions.

Funny stuff huh?

But racist.

In another episode the father has been given a promotion at work, only to realize he has been appointed as his company's first black senior vice president of the "urban" division. Urban meaning black. His reaction is frustration, obviously recognizing that black stereotypes are once again being used by whites.

In another episode, the grandfather, played by Laurence Fishburne, remarks, "I told you so" when the family's children seemed to neither know or care that Barack Obama was the first black President of the United States.

All of it funny, but racist as racist can be.

Donald Trump, came out publicly calling the show racist, writing, "How is ABC television allowed to have a show entitled, 'Blackish?' Can you imagine a show called, 'Whiteish?' Racism at the highest level." Now I am not a Donald Trump fan, but right on Donald!

The creator of the show, Kenya Barris responded to Trump's a(
with an interesting comment in the Hollywood Reporter about why)
that title, "Instead of calling it 'The Burbs' or 'New Rules' or somethi,
that, we wanted to reflect that this is the world we are living in."

The interesting part is his choice of the phrase, "... the world we are living in."

What world is that Mr. Barris? A world which is so stricken with a politically-mindset of reverse discrimination and where blacks are pandered to so much that you know you can openly use such a racist name as "Blackish" and there isn't a thing the silent white majority can do about it?

Or ask popular country music artist Brad Paisley about being labeled a 'racist' for the joke he told about "Blackish" on the CMA Awards show in late fall of 2014.

The CMAs were aired in the time slot normally held by "Blackish" on ABC. Paisley welcomed guests back to the CMAs from a commercial with this line-- "Everybody, there's usually a show on Wednesdays—a new show I've fallen in love with. It's so funny. And if any of you tuned in to ABC tonight expecting to see the new show "Blackish," yeah.... this ain't it." He added, while gesturing at himself and the predominantly white country music crowd, "In the meantime I hope you enjoy 'White—ish.'"

Twitter went wild with accusations that Paisley was a racist.

But is that racist?

No. Or at least no more than the name of the show he was joking about.

He didn't create the name for the show "Blackish." He was just poking fun at it, and probably even at the country music world for being so 'white.'

So for anyone to dare accuse Paisley of being a racist but not acknowledge the sitcom as racist in turn is about as two-faced as two-faced can be.

But once again that double standard is encouraged by the mindset of reverse discrimination that exists, and which seems to grow stronger and stronger with the passing of time, such that blacks and NBC can so blatantly give a sitcom such a racist name, and send it into the living rooms of whites every Wednesday night, and whites can't even make a joke about it in return.

And how do you think a show called "Whiteish" would be accepted?

Imagine a white family living in the hood. The white father is afraid that his white children are losing touch with their White American Heritage.

The son comes home one day and wants to try out some of that Church's fried chicken because all of his black buddies at school go there for lunch.

Or maybe the white teenage daughter comes home from high school one day and tells how she knows that she is finally Jamaal's girlfriend, because he called her 'bitch' and 'hoe,' and slapped her a time or two that day at school.

Or the white grandfather comes into the house as happy as can be, because all of his black checker playing buddies from the park called him 'nigga' and said he could use that term of endearment in referring to each of them.

The father is appalled, "We can't do that! We're white!"

How would all of that play out in a sitcom called "Whiteish" on ABC or CBS, every Thursday night?

You know these other main networks probably are jealous of NBC's "Blackish" and would love to have similar shows of their own.

No?

Make that a hell no.

Chapter 17: "The Oscars Are Too White"

It's the 18th of January, 2015, the eve of Dr. Martin Luther King, Jr Day as I write this chapter. I peruse the internet and come across a story about where Al Sharpton, who seems to be the best, but at the same time, the worst possible torch bearer of the civil rights movement, has criticized the Academy Awards, the Oscars, for being, "too white."

I think back to Dr Martin Luther King, Jr. and his role in history, and how he seemed to be able to not only pick the right battles, but how he had a cunning ability to pick the right battles at just the right time.

You may not know it but Rosa Parks was NOT the first black person to refuse to give up her seat to a white on a Montgomery, Alabama bus in the 1960's.

Early on a young black girl named Claudette Colvin had been the first black person to do so, her defiance occurring nine months prior to that of Rosa Parks. Colvin was only 15 at the time.

However, it was felt by black leaders of the day that Colvin was too young, and too dark skinned to be an effective symbol of injustice for the nation.

It was further discovered that the young lady was pregnant out of wedlock, by a married man, a storyline which would not have played well at the time. So they decided to wait.

Nine months later, Rosa Parks came along, and as you know, and as they so commonly say, "the rest is history."

But here we are, just a short time after Ferguson and Michael Brown, after Staten Island and Eric Garner, and all of the uproar and media support those stories have given the black cause and Sharpton is calling the Oscars too white?

Seriously?

He is basing this on the fact that out of all the leading and supporting actor nominations which have just been released for the 2015 version, not a single one was black.

The civil rights era movie 'Selma' did, however, garner a best picture nomination.

Further his accusation comes only a year after 'Twelve Years a Slave' WON the best picture award at the Oscars, and Lupita Nyong'o WON for best supporting actress.

He even has called for a meeting of his 'diversity task force' to decide the next action to take. Really? Whites everywhere must be shaking in their boots!

Come on Al. Is that all you've got?

Are you really wanting to make the Oscars the next great battle in the new civil rights movement?

And does your line of reasoning then make the NBA look "too black?" Because on any given night in any given NBA game, I would almost bet that at least eight or nine out of ten players on the floor are black. College hoops and even professional and college football are the same.

According to your train of thought, it does. If the Oscars are "too white" then professional and college basketball and football are "too black."

Haven't yet heard anyone make that claim, now have ya?

But again because the politically-correct mindset of reverse discrimination and the excessive pandering to blacks, society is only allowed to assume there is discrimination when it's whites against blacks but not when it's blacks against whites.

So we are not really supposed to go down that road are we?

But griping about the Oscar nominations?

Really?

How about dealing with the cold hard facts of poverty and education, and social-economic status for blacks and how that contributes to huge numbers of black unemployment and disproportional numbers by percentage of blacks on welfare.

What about facts like roughly 67 percent of black children are raised in single parent (mother) homes, many percentages higher than for whites and other races.

Deal with those things Al, and perhaps the plight of blacks will improve.

I have my own theory about why 'Selma' might not have gotten the critical acclaim it deserves. And I will state it in the form of a question.

Could it be a backlash from the force fed, media hyped, so-called new civil rights movement, being based on the likes of Al Sharpton, and thugs like Micheal Brown and his step father Louis Head, and consisting of all the violence, as opposed to the non-violent peaceful accomplishments of the real Civil Rights Movement of the days of Dr. King?

Perhaps that is precisely the answer.

To begin with, I watched 'Selma' and thought it to be a great movie. It is deserving of a best picture nod and could win. (It didn't though) And I felt that David Oleyowo, who portrayed MLK, should have been nominated for best actor, and even Carmen Ejogo, for her portrayal of Coretta Scott King should have been nominated for at least a supporting role.

But look at what has been happening.

Riots and violence and protest over the grand jury finding in Ferguson.

I, for one, thought the grand jury was correct in not indicting officer Darren Wilson for the shooting death of Michael Brown.

And I would venture a guess that most of the whites in America, and perhaps many of the Oscar voters, feel the same way.

Again, Michael Brown had just committed at least two felonies, including bitch-slapping a store owner in a robbery just a few minutes before he was shot, and in assaulting a police officer by grabbing his gun.

But society and the media allowed the shooting death to become a 'black versus white' thing.

It's a world of black pandering, remember?

I am sorry, but remember my 'right battles at the right times' reference above about MLK? Choosing Michael Brown, a criminal, a thug, (a chapter on 'thug mentality' is herein) as a person on which to base a cause is NOT, repeat NOT, the right battle.

Again, however, the media and society allowed it to be assumed that there must have been discrimination, and Ferguson was thereafter and continually and literally crammed down people's throats, including white people's throats, and again, those Oscar voters.

Now I do want to add that the later choke-hold death of Eric Garner could have maybe, just maybe salvaged any kind of traction, because I for one thought that officer Daniel Pantaleo should have been indicted for that death. And for a moment it looked like the' black versus white thing' might be turned into a 'people versus bad cop' thing.

But alas, Sharpton and his cronies and the media continued to lump the two together in their "hands up, don't shoot," "black lives matter" crusade.

Violence continued to be a part of the norm, regardless of whether CBS News and CNN and other media outlets put very many stories about that violence on their websites or into the living rooms of America.

And citizens were presented none of those stories about where whites were being killed by blacks, and black cops, etc. etc.

Thus, I feel a large and silent (I want to steer clear of just saying 'white' here) majority perhaps did, and do not, see the makings of a new civil right movement, especially if it's going to be based on the likes of Al Sharpton, Michael Brown (not Garner), and chants of, "burn this bitch down."

And then from there we hear that the Oscars are too white?

No wonder that many whites and even some black writers are trying to distance the black movement away from Al Sharpton.

Some writers are even outright suggesting that any new civil rights movement is basing itself in young blacks, who are not falling in lockstep with Sharpton.

In any event, it has become politically-correct to give Sharpton and his followers or these other young protestors the time of day. Society allows it, as the pandering continues.

We see very few reasoned others allowed on the news shows, other than Fox, to give opinions of why the grand jury decision of Ferguson just might have been correct.

Instead, society can assume it was wrong and just another case where white has discriminated against black.

Now, to conclude my theory on why the Oscars this year are too "white?"

Maybe, just maybe, some of society, (refer to the above) is getting to the point of having simply had enough.

Charles G. Ankrom

Any proof you ask? Perhaps.

'Selma' was an excellent movie, as good or even better than 'Twelve Years a Slave' but got only one nomination for the Academy Awards!

Chapter 18: Obama and the Rodeo Clown

In case you missed it, there was a supposed 'incident' at the Missouri State Fair (my home state by the way) in Sedalia, Missouri on August 11, 2013 in which a rodeo clown put on an Obama mask and brought the house down when it was asked by the clown or the announcer, (it's not entirely clear from the videos exeactly who said it) if anyone wanted to see Obama run down by a bull.

A picture of the same seemed to make all the various national and local media outlets. Go look it up.

"We're gonna smoke Obama. Obama they're coming for you this time. Don't you move, he's gonna getcha, getcha, getcha, getcha!"

Further taunting that, "Obama's just gonna have to stay there. Obama watch out for those bulls," the dialogue went on.

Have comedians not made fun of presidents forever, or at least all the way back to comedian Bob Hope about the presidents of his day?

How many of us laughed as Chevy Chase stumbled around the 'oval' office impersonating then President Gerald Ford and finally stumbled onto the nuclear war button, only to jump up and proclaim, "Live from New York, it's Saturday Night?"

Or how about the portrayal of President Nixon with the flabby jowls?

It 's a part of Americana, for goodness sakes, for comedians to make fun of presidents. They have done it for years, and nobody ever seems to complain.

They just laugh.

Charles G. Ankrom

I mean, President Obama is clearly not the first president for which a masked likeness has been made.

Masks of presidents, and other celebrities for that matter, end up on store shelves for Halloween costumes each and every year.

And perhaps you can remember comedian Steve Bridges, who made a living portraying George W Bush in all his clumsiness?

And how he made it appear that Bush was so inept at speaking, to the point of actually making "W" look dumb?

Comedians from Leno to Letterman and the cast of Saturday Night Live on down have forever cracked jokes in skits and otherwise about the sitting president and presidents past.

In fact, Saturday Night Live seems to have made it a policy to always have an actor-comedian on staff who could portray the sitting president.

Nothing has ever been said, that I know of, condemning this practice or any of this joking by comedians about presidents for the past five decades.

Until now, that is, And never to the degree to which the rodeo clown in Missouri took a hit.

The name of the rodeo clown, whose name was withheld from the public for a short time during all the fiasco because of death threats, is Tuffy Gessling. He is a veteran of the rodeo clown circuit and has poked fun at Presidents Bush, Clinton, and Ronald Reagan.

As a result of his Obama anitcs, however, Gessling was banned forever from the Missouri State Fair.

Pandering to blacks, you think?

Wait, there's a whole lot more.

The Missouri Rodeo Clown's Association's contract with the Missouri State Fair was being reviewed at the time this was written, and personnel and performers from then on were required to undergo 'sensitivity training' if they were to ever work at the fair again.

In addition, the rodeo announcer, who was also president of the Missouri Association of Rodeo Clowns (and also superintendent of the Boonville, Missouri schools) resigned his position.

Apologies were issued far and wide, from the fair association to the rodeo clown association, from Missouri Governor Jay Nixon, a Democrat, to Missouri Lieutenant Governor Peter Kinder, a Republican. One Senator from Missouri, Claire McCaskill, also a Democrat, called the 'incident' "disrespectful" and "unacceptable."

Some even used the 'incident' to question state funding for the Missouri State Fair which has always been considered a family event and one of the better state fairs in the nation.

Missouri Rep. Steve Webb called on the Governor to cancel the Governor's Ham Breakfast which was scheduled for later in the week.

He was quoted in the Kansas City Star as saying, "Since I've been in the legislature, we have seen a lot of things with racial undertones. But nothing's ever done about it. There has to be consequences at some point," obviously implying, I suppose, that this 'incident' was racial simply because of the fact it was a black Obama clown being made fun of in front of a predominantly white crowd.

That alone makes it racial?

I guess it does when society automatically presumes discrimination of blacks by whites, according to the politically-correct mindset of reverse discrimination, along with the excessive pandering to blacks.

One Tea Party talk show host, Dana Loesch seemed to get to that point by saying that, "any mocking, any ridicule, is reflexively racist."

Yeah, my point exactly. Society has made it a reflex to presume discrimination by whites against blacks!

This 'incident' was reported in all the major media sources. Liberal bloggers and websites immediately denounced the 'incident' as racial.

It was also reported in media outlets that one spectator, a Perry Beam, likened the incident to "an effigy at a Klan rally."

Really?

A Klan rally?

I bet all those people, along with their children at the Missouri State Fair, missed that one!

Beam told the St Louis Post Dispatch, "I've never seen anything so blatantly racist in my life."

And then the bomb dropped.

The Missouri Chapter of the NAACP issued this statement, through their state president Mary Ratliff, "The activities at the Missouri State Fair targeting and inciting violence against our President are serious and warrant a full review by both the Secret Service and Department of Justice."

Unbelievable.

A call for the Department of Justice to investigate a rodeo clown wearing an Obama mask?

This, at a time when there were cries from every corner of the public for a full review by the same Department of Justice for the terrorist killings of our American ambassador in Benghazi and three other personnel, which had just recently happened.

And here is the NAACP wanting a full investigation of a rodeo clown wearing an Obama mask?

How could it even come to this?

Just saying it—a rodeo clown wearing an Obama mask—sounds silly.

How could the mindset of our society have even gotten to this point of absurdity?

How could the pandering of blacks have gotten to such a level?

A politically-correct mindset of reverse discrimination, that's how.

An ingrained presumption, accepted by society, of discrimination of blacks by whites in any setting where a black has supposedly been wronged, and there are whites on the other 'side' just fit for the blaming.

Now the real question, that lends to my book's premise, is why was this even an 'incident' at all? And especially considering that comedians have poked fun at presidents since the days of Bob Hope.

Why was it so widely reported, and why in the world was it automatically allowed to be viewed as racial?

In fact, other than another clown supposedly running up and flapping the clown's lips (I wonder who made the mask) and even then you have to buy into another black stereotype, nothing at all can be viewed as racial, aside of the fact that the rodeo clown was white (which you couldn't see under the mask by the way) and that Obama is black.

I invite you to look up the videos posted on YouTube and tell me one thing that makes this 'incident' racial, other than possibly the flapping of the clown's lips.

There has been virtually no backlash for other comedians trashing the presidents of the past for some 50 years.

But President Obama is off limits and the only reason there can be for that is that he is black.

Society is, and has reached an epic point of pandering to blacks, if you ask me.

Now oddly, Mr Beam, when interviewed by NBC Action News in a clip that aired on NBC affiliate channel 41 in Macon, Georgia did not include in this television interview version that another clown had ran up and flapped the lips on the Obama mask.

This came later by Beam in a posting on Facebook. Now, maybe there's nothing to that, but odd, don't you think, that the only thing other than the mask being of a black Obama that could arguably make the incident racial is the flapping of the mask lips. And odd because it wasn't until later that the lip-flapping claim was even mentioned. And, again, even calling the lip-flapping racial is a stretch.

Once again, here is yet another example where something not racial is allowed to be looked at as racial by society, at least as far as discrimination of blacks by whites and the way it's presumed to exist.

And oh, by the way, there was a story about another rodeo clown making a comeback in 1994 in the Philadelphia Inquirer that described one of the young man's stunts as wearing a George Bush (Sr.) mask as a rodeo clown and letting the bull run over him and send the mask flying.

No one called that an 'incident.'

And I bet you didn' t hear anything about that being 'disrespectful' or 'unacceptable' either.

No apologies by governors or senators. No statements by the NAACP or any similar white group, no one losing their job over it, etc, In fact, very little news coverage at all.

Nothing.

And by now, you know the story!

Chapter 19: The Harlem Globetrotters

Would he dare attack the Harlem Globetrotters, you ask?

Well,......... yeah, because a game I watched them 'play' or more appropriately 'perform' in, back in the late 90's is where the formation of the actual idea for this book came about.

Now by way of disclaimer, and to be fair to the Globetrotters, I have seen a portion of their show recently and they seem to have cleaned up their act, at least as far as some of the spoken lines and racial jokes. The innuendos, however, are still there.

President Harry S. Truman, yes a fellow Missourian, called the Harlem Globetrotters "Ambassadors of Goodwill" and even allowed his administration to assist the team on their world tour in 1952.

They have performed for literally millions in many countries around the world. For presidents, world leaders, famous people, and even royalty, even the Pope. Entertaining and funny they are.

But did you ever watch the Globetrotters, and take a moment to seriously study, or consider their humor? At least during the early years and even up into the 90's?

I did.

It was in Springfield, Missouri in the late 1990's.

They 'played' a game, if you could call it that, against the Washington Generals, a traveling team of all white players, that traveled with the Globetrotters back then. I think they still do, but the team of Generals has added some black players to the roster, something I feel is a smart move.

Charles G. Ankrom

It is kind of hard to find any white Harlem Globetrotters. There have only been three, and even this seems to support this chapter about the Harlem Globetrotters as racists.

But back in the 90's the Generals were all white and part of the entire Globetrotter repertoire was for the Generals to stumble slowly around, looking even somewhat stupid, just so that the Globetrotters could make fun of them and look amazing, And that they did. And society loved em.

Still do.

Now Springfield, Missouri happens to be the second 'whitest' city in the nation, behind Portland, Oregon, of cities with populations of over 100,000 people. According to the latest census in 2010, only 4.1 percent of the population of Springfield was black.

So here we were, sitting in Hammons Student Center on the campus of Southwest Missouri State University (now Missouri State University) with a crowd of about 7500 people, which was probably at least 95 percent white, if not more. So, an almost all-white crowd to say the least.

The Harlem Globetrotters, whose players were all black came out on the floor.

Now I've got to say that from the start they were very entertaining and funny and the almost all-white crowd roared with laughter along with myself.

But me? Being a young white guy from the Midwest with the subject matter of this book already floating around in my head from watching the 1992 movie, "White Men Can't Jump." began to notice something—these guys were racists, plain and simple.

Meadowlark Lemon went into the crowd, (the Globetrotters were very good at interacting with the crowd, I have to say) and borrowed a dorky-looking ladies hat to wear around for a bit on the floor.

He proceeded to go back into the crowd to return the hat but seemed to have lost track of where the lady he had gotten it from was sitting. "Gosh you people all look alike," he said.

Total laughter.

But totally racist, at least if the same had been said by a white player in an all-black crowd.

In fact most, if not all, of the jokes seemed racist.

Curly Lemon dribbled his way through several oaf-looking white Generals' players, winding up humiliating a small white player by appearing to dribble the ball straight out of bounds only to stuff it in the jersey of the ignorant acting white player just before going out of bounds, the momentum of the white player propelling him awkwardly into the first row of seats.

"Out of bounds, Globetrotters ball," roared the referee, followed by the roar of the crowd.

White players were made to appear slow and told as much, "Gosh you white guys ARE slow," said the Globetrotters, with the emphasis on ARE.

Even the referees, who were white, were ridiculed, and openly made fun of by Meadowlark as, "That little white guy,"

At one point the white referee also chased Curly around as he was dribbling. Curly stopped at the out of bounds line, but the referee continued, half stumbling his way into the third row of bleachers.

The crowd roared again.

Racist joke after racist joke.

Nothing but laughter from the crowd.

Charles G. Ankrom

And so it was here at this very Harlem Globetrotters game, that my second true inspiration for writing this book came about.

Now, as indicated, at first I wondered why no one had thought the movie 'White Men Can't Jump' was racist when it came out back in 1992.

And now here I wondered why no one, other than me, thought that the antics of the Globetrotters were racist.

But something about it was even worse--not only did this crowd fail to see the Globetrotters as racist, they didn't even remotely, or even slightly see them as such.

Society just didn't care I surmised.

Society was blind.

Or had society just been programmed to this politically-correct mindset of reverse discrimination even as far back as the 1990's?

Blacks could make fun of whites all they wanted to, or at least the Harlem Globetrotters could. And it seemed to be the norm of society. The rule.

Accepted.

The black antics of the Globetrotters were pandered to, by an adoring society.

Even popular, when one took into account the popularity of the Harlem Globetrotters.

I sat and wondered if the opposite could ever be true.

Would it ever be allowed for a white basketball team, or wait, maybe a white tennis team, or a white golf team, (this was before Tiger Woods) to openly make fun of the inability of blacks to play the game?

No way. I thought.

"Black Men Can't Play Tennis?" "Black Men Can't Golf?" Such would clearly be struck down as racist.

My thinking switched from a sports scenario to something from the educational field, thinking a title for a fictional movie which contained something along the lines of "Black Men Can't Read" would be even more thought provoking.

More controversial?

For sure.

But in being more controversial, perhaps there was an even better chance for the idea of a politically-correct mindset of reverse discrimination to be presented.

So there in Section M, row 24, seat 17, the idea, and planning, for this book and it's opening supposition of a fictional movie similar to "White Men Can't Jump" except with the roles reversed was seriously considered for the first time.

Who knows, I thought at the time. The situation might get better, not worse. Perhaps the good in all people would prevail. That niceness and equality might become the rule of the day.

But as time passed, boy did I ever realize how wrong I was!

Chapter 20: Reparations

Surely blacks are joking about this one?

Right?

Well, maybe not.

Reparations is the idea that some sort of compensation should be made by the government to the descendants of enslaved black people in the United States, in consideration of the coerced, and hence, uncompensated, labor of their ancestors under the institution of slavery.

It appears this notion originated with some antiquated Special Field Order 15 which was issued by Northern General Tecumseh Sherman after the end of the Civil War which proposed giving, "forty acres of tillable land" around Charleston, South Carolina, to each freed family of former slaves.

Some freed families did receive the 40 acres, and a mule, as there was an abundance of mules after the war.

The order, however, was rescinded by President Andrew Johnson after President Lincoln's assassination, and the land was returned to the original owners.

I am not sure what happened to the mules!

I, for one, think this is the most ridiculous idea ever, and complete nonsense and shouldn't even be given the time of day!

Again, any idea to ever think seriously about reparations had to be a joke.

Why should I, or more accurately my taxes, have to pay for something my ancestors may or may not have done over a hundred fifty years ago, to people that are no longer around?

Surely this idea wouldn't be even remotely considered today, would it?

Afraid so.

Blacks are pandered to, according to the politically-correct mindset of reverse discrimination.

There was a proposal for reparations made at the first National Reparations Convention convened at the McCormick Convention Center in Chicago in 2004, by Howshua Amariel, an activist from Chicago, which would require the federal government to fork over to proven descendants of slaves, "free education, free medical, free legal and free financial aid for 50 years with no taxes levied."

Why just 50 years, I want to sarcastically ask.

And what happened to the 40 acres and a mule?

Various estimates for total 'reparations' under Amariel's plan, which got 100 votes at the convention, exceed $100 trillion, yes, trillion, dollars.

It's hard to even seriously write about this issue, but guess what?

On July 30, 2008, the United States House of Representatives did pass a resolution apologizing for, "American slavery and subsequent discriminatory laws."

The states of Virginia, Maryland, and North Carolina have also apologized.

And William 'Sandy' Darity, a professor from Duke University, has said such apologies are a first step, but that compensation is necessary.

Now I don't know how you feel about it, but in the legal world an apology is the same thing as an admission.

So, U.S. House of Representatives, and Virginia, Maryland and North Carolina, stop exposing our tax dollars to the most ridiculous idea I have ever heard.

And it doesn't end there.

There have been actual lawsuits filed against corporations which were actually involved in slavery.

None of these suits have yet to be successful, however, a federal court has left the door open for them to be, although it has established substantial procedural and substantive hurdles that plaintiffs must clear first.

Companies which have apologized for slavery include JP Morgan, Aetna, and Wachovia.

California, which always seems to have the need to add their two cents worth, added their two cents worth in 2000, by passing a Slavery Era Disclosure Law, which requires insurance companies doing business in California to disclose their role in slavery.

This same law, or laws similar to it have passed in 12 other states.

In 1995, The Southern Baptist Convention apologized for the "sins" of slavery.

And of course, the NAACP jumped all over this one too. The say, "Absolutely, we will be pursuing reparations from companies that have historical ties to slavery and will be engaging all parties to come to the table."

Blacks cite that precedent exists for 'reparations' for slavery in that the United States government did compensate Japanese American who were interred during World War II, under the provisions of the Civil Liberties Act of 1988.

Further they cite the fact that Native American Indians have received compensation for lands ceded to the United States under various treaties.

One argument against 'reparations' seems to be that only a small percentage of Southern whites and even a smaller percent of all whites (only about one and a half percent) were actually responsible for slavery.

Many people do not even realize that many of the Southern slave owners were, in fact, BLACK! Even the very FIRST recorded slave owner in America was BLACK!. Look it up.

So why should all Americans bear the burden?

Also, and what I feel is the best argument against 'reparations' is the fact that, during the time slavery was widely used, slavery was still legal. It wasn't until the Thirteenth Amendment to the United States Constitution in 1865 that the institution of slavery became illegal.

There also exist other legal arguments against 'reparations' such as Statute of Limitations, and the fact that the United States didn't even exist until the Constitution was ratified in 1788 meaning the United States was NOT responsible for the bringing over of slaves and the establishment of slavery. They just inherited the problem.

Further, it's argued that an identification of the actual descendants of slavery would be next to impossible. To coin the phrase of Meadowlark Lemon of the Harlem Globetrotters, and which could get me in trouble but here goes, "they all look alike."

I didn't actually say that did I?

Black Pandering

You know what? Yes I did. Because if Meadowlark Lemon can say that jokingly about whites then I should be allowed to say that jokingly about blacks.

In any event, any talk of 'reparations' should be nothing but a joke, but unfortunately, with all the apologies left and right I probably should inform you that because of the politically-correct mindset of reverse discrimination which exists in our society, and the excessive pandering of blacks, the dialogue is, in fact, real.

I can just about guarantee one thing.

If any dollars are ever paid to any blacks compensating them for the slavery of the past, there will be a revolt in this country the likes of which has never been seen.

I wonder if I should propose 'reparations' for white Americans, or their families, who have been the victims of black murders, rapes, and other crimes committed during the last few decades or so, considering the hugely disproportionate number of crimes committed by blacks compared to the number of crimes committed by whites?

No?

Ok, I didn't think so either.

That would be racist!

Chapter 21: And Then Along Came Trayvon

I knew you would expect this chapter in this book about this subject.

So here it is.

I had actually gotten to a point in writing the book, having completed roughly one-third of it, when I sort of bogged down. That was in January of 2013. I had laid it aside, scolding myself from time to time for not picking it back up and finishing it.

Then on July 13, 2013 the decision came down in the George Zimmerman case. Or wait a minute, the Trayvon Martin case, all depending on which camp you were in and which news station, Fox or CNN you listened to the most.

Never before had I seen the media (and listeners, herds of cattle if you will) so divided on the racial issue. Or any issue for that matter.

The pandering of blacks in America had truly reached epic proportions.

Coverage on CNN was calling it the Trayvon Martin case. Andersen Cooper quickly had a town hall panel show called "Race and Justice in America" airing several times a week. All of his guests were voicing their opinions about how wrong the not guilty verdict was. Their coverage was heavily slanted along the lines that the jury had obviously made a mistake and the reason for mistake was just as obvious—RACE!

Perhaps a mindset of reverse discrimination? Yep.

Protests were held in many major cities, something like over one hundred cities promoting "Justice for Trayvon."

And did the media show up? You bet.

Al Sharpton and Jesse Jackson, true to form, also showed up. Why, a young black unarmed teenager had been murdered and his white killer was set free, and free indeed, or so it was told.

Here's the problem with all of that, as even admitted to by the jurors themselves--Race was not even slightly involved in the case.

At all!

In fact, an actual juror in the case, Juror B-29, appeared on the "Good Morning America" show a few days after the verdict and told the interviewer that race was not even discussed in the deliberations. Another actual juror in the case, Juror B-37 also had made statements that race had not been discussed in the deliberations.

Good gosh, the defining fact of the entire matter, and the fact that most proves the point of a politically-correct mindset of reverse discrimination and black pandering is that George Zimmerman was NOT EVEN WHITE!

He was Hispanic.

Apparently, the Associated Press had reported on March 8, 2012 that the neighborhood watchman was "white."

CNN actually either created, or at least used the most, the term "White Hispanic" for the duration of the case to even be able to suggest the case was about race at all.

And use it they did. And all of the media, except Fox, followed.

And worse yet, and it goes to prove the point of my book, most all of America allowed them to do this.

It was politically-correct for the media to make this case totally about race and use it as a spark plug to ignite racial protests all over the country,

Black Pandering

despite what the jurors and everyone associated with the actual case (lawyers, witnesses, and court personnel) had to say.

In actuality George Zimmerman is no more white than President Obama. And have you ever heard anyone refer to him as a White Black person?

Come on people!

All one has to do is examine how CNN handled coverage from the start to see how they fed all of America the entire case as a racial injustice.

To begin with, when the shooting occurred, the picture of Trayvon Martin which was used was that of a smiling baby-faced teenage boy, I think he was 14 in the picture used. It was not a picture of him at 17 in a dark colored hoodie as was the case on that fateful night.

And the picture of George Zimmerman was of him from a mug shot years earlier, not of the young man in a suit who had been picked by his neighborhood and peers to coordinate the neighborhood watch program in his subdivision, which seemed to more accurately depict his character.

Blacks everywhere jumped on the bandwagon early on as every update on the case seemed to suggest the shooting was racially motivated.

Interestingly, I was watching CNN a short time after the verdict, on August 26, 2013, where anchor Suzanne Malveaux reported about a separate case, the arrest of two black teenagers in the beating death of a white World War II veteran in Spokane, Washington.

At the end of her report she added, "Police say there is no evidence the attack was racially motivated." O.K. Fine. But why did she make it a point to add that to the story at all?

And even better still, or worse yet, depending on your point of view, why wasn't that added to any of the stories about Trayvon Martin/George

Zimmerman case? I don't recall CNN ever reporting that the Trayvon Martin/George Zimmerman case was NOT about race.

In fact, as detailed above, CNN and other media did exactly the opposite and played it to the hilt that it WAS racially motivated.

And again, as referenced herein, there was no evidence, either initially, or ever for that matter, to even suggest (remember the two jurors) that race was involved in the Trayvon Martin/George Zimmerman case.

So why the difference?

It's simply the politically-correct mindset of reverse discrimination that exists, which permeates our society. And because of this mindset, society allows it to simply be presumed there is discrimination of blacks by whites, as blacks who cry racism are pandered to.

Once the trial began, CNN's primary news reporters were both black.

Seriously.!

Couldn't they put one white reporter on the case? Just one? Or how about a Hispanic? Maybe even a 'White Hispanic?'

And both of the black reporters on the case seemed to criticize the defense from the get-go, suggesting that a guilty verdict certainly had to be in order.

I guess my big problem with all this was how had our society gotten to the point that a case which was not about race at all, could so blatantly be treated like it was in the media coverage.

It became so obvious to me that our society had so deeply adopted a mindset of reverse discrimination, and to such a degree that all the actual facts and evidence were simply ignored.

Blacks and the media had an agenda. And it was an agenda that society allowed and perpetuated. Discrimination of whites against blacks was simply going to be presumed in our society, and in this case, even when it was clear that the person involved was Hispanic, and no more white than Obama.

Now how many of you ever heard of the John McNeil case that was occurring in Georgia at about the same time, or a year or so earlier than the Trayvon Martin/George Zimmerman case?

Go look it up.

That was a case where a black man, John McNeil had shot and killed a white man, Brian Epp, who was trespassing in his yard. McNeil's teenage son had apparently called McNeil about a stranger lurking about their property.

Sound familiar?

It's the Trayvon Martin/George Zimmerman case in reverse. You might be thinking that it surely had to turn out similar to the Trayvon Martin/George Zimmerman case, right? That society could presume that the black man was discriminating against the white one and just shot him, all due to some racial motivation.

Right?

Wrong.

Totally.

In fact, in that case McNeil, the black man, was charged and convicted of killing Epp, the white man and sentenced to life imprisonment. And oddly enough the NAACP jumped on exactly the opposite side of the exact same factual situation as Trayvon Martin/George Zimmerman and rallied to have McNeil, the black man who had been convicted, set free.

I guess it's all about the color to the NAACP.

But you didn't hear about that one did you?

Probably not when it happened. And oddly enough, you probably didn't even hear about it during the Trayvon Martin/George Zimmerman case.

Why not?

The cities where these two similar events and cases happened are less than 500 miles apart, in adjoining states, and only a short hop by airplane. The facts are very similar, almost the same, except for the fact that the races are opposite.

So any coverage of the Trayvon Martin/George Zimmerman case would surely reference a case close in proximity, with similar facts where the race roles were reversed? Right?

Nope.

There was no way the American public would ever hear about the McNeil/Epp case, in conjunction with Trayvon Martin/George Zimmerman.

And why?

Because with the mindset of reverse discrimination and the pandering of blacks, discrimination only goes one way.

And even though the cases were so similar in facts and so close together physically and in time, they were always a million miles apart.

Looking back on those two cases there is another reason, an even better one, why the McNeil/Epp case should have been looked at alongside the Trayvon Martin/George Zimmerman case.

This reason involves the fact that the result in both cases hinged on the interpretation of the self-defense laws of each state involved—Florida for Trayvon Martin/George Zimmerman, Georgia for McNeil/Epp.

Perhaps thrown into that mix could have also been a discussion of a case in New York from 2009 where another black man, Roderick Scott, had shot and killed a white man Christopher Cervini, whom Scott thought was burglarizing a neighbor's car.

This case was also eerily similar to the Trayvon Martin/George Zimmerman and McNeil/Epp cases, expect again for the reversal of the races of the parties just like in the McNeil/Epp case.

But America also never heard of any comparisons of Trayvon Martin/George Zimmerman to the Scott/Cervini case either, even though its ruling ALSO hinged on the interpretation of New York's self-defense law which was somewhat different than that of Florida and Georgia.

In Florida and Georgia the principal of self defense was 'stand your ground,' meaning that a person had no duty to retreat from any place they had the legal right to be, and could use any level of force, even lethal, if they reasonably believed they faced an imminent and immediate threat of serious bodily harm or death.

In New York the self-defense law was that a person was entitled to defend his home or even outside of it if he believed that his life was in imminent danger AND retreat was not an option.

It would have actually made for good news reporting, and good journalism would seem to require stories or articles comparing the self-defense laws of all of these states, or more particularly comparing how they were applied in these similar cases in these states, all occurring at roughly the same, or similar, time.

And especially, when considering that one result of the Trayvon Martin/George Zimmerman verdict was a huge public outcry, mostly from blacks and black groups, for Florida and other states to rethink their self-defense laws, you would have for sure thought that any media discussions would have included all three cases.

But even though the coverage of all three cases would have seemed to make good journalism sense, there was no way that was going to happen.

Ever.

Because of the politically-correct mindset of reverse discrimination.

The Trayvon Martin/George Zimmerman story was a racial injustice story, plain and simple, and a racial injustice story only, and America was not about to hear about any cases where whites had been shot by blacks.

But do the facts and figures support my claim that the media hyped the Trayvon Martin/George Zimmerman case as racial?

Let's look, for instance at NPR. National Public Radio. Fair reporting? What are the numbers? In an article on NewsBusters, author John Williams says that on NPR, a full 259 separate pieces about the case were on air over a 16-month period. 190 of those mentioned, or about 80 percent, used the word 'black.'

And 16 articles specifically referred to Trayvon Martin as an 'unarmed black teenager'. Yet in only 15 percent of those 190 articles was the words 'Hispanic' or 'Latino' even used, with only 5 articles (3 percent) calling George Zimmerman simply "Hispanic' or 'Latino'.

Michel Martin, of NPR in her news and talk program, 'Tell Me More,' regularly referred to George Zimmerman as a "white Hispanic," "white and of Hispanic heritage," or that his "father is white."

And more specifically, she said of Zimmerman, "His family tells us he identifies as Hispanic, but many people sort of see him as white."

You have got to be kidding me.

I thought NPR was supposed to be fair. Yet the presumption of discrimination of blacks by whites (reverse discrimination) and the pandering of blacks, was clearly accepted, even by a news organization as trustworthy as NPR.

Keith Woods, NPR's Vice President for Diversity in News, said of Zimmerman's race, "He's a, you know, he's a white man."

Of Zimmerman being born to a Peruvian mother he added, "Does that make him Latino? What does that have to do, in the end, with the racial angle of this story?"

So here is a quote from a journalist admitting how his news organization did, in fact, create a "racial angle" to the Trayvon Martin/George Zimmerman case.

And for the kicker, NPR actually has a full RACE desk, alongside its foreign and crime desks for reporting. Oh, and not to mention, according to Williams, is that NPR received a $1.5 million grant from the Corporation for Public Broadcasting to set up said RACE desk.

Imagine that. Federal Funding to promote the creation of race 'angled' (blacks being discriminated against by whites) stories to feed to the American public.

In order to be fully versed on the Trayvon Martin/George Zimmerman case, a little of the factual background is crucial.

Both Zimmerman and Martin were living, or staying at a 260 unit residential complex called the Retreat at Twin Lakes in Sanford, Florida.

In a little over a year prior to the shooting, the Sanford police had been called to the Retreat a total of 401 times. There had been eight burglaries, nine thefts, and one shooting during that time.

In September of 2011, the residents met to form a neighborhood watch and Zimmerman was selected as its coordinator.

During the few months prior to the shooting Zimmerman had called the police several times reporting suspicious behavior of individuals, and just three weeks prior to the shooting one of his calls to the police were about a young male allegedly peering into windows in the neighborhood.

Other workers in the development had noticed, around that time, two black males lingering in a yard on the same day that several items were reported stolen from that home.

On the day of the shooting itself, Zimmerman was actually driving around on patrol and noticed, and reported to police a young man, Trayvon Martin who was just walking around looking at houses.

Zimmerman reported to the police that the man was running and that he attempted to follow Martin but lost him. The police asked if Zimmerman was following the man, and Zimmerman said, "yeah." The dispatcher told Zimmerman that he didn't have to do that.

It was at that point that the confrontation happened where Zimmerman shot Martin, in a spot in the neighborhood in the back yards of some of the residences, or away from the streets of the neighborhood.

Zimmerman was taken into custody for questioning, with a bloody nose and abrasions on the back of his head, and questioned for five hours. Then he was let go.

Bill Lee, police chief for the Sanford Police Department, who would resign his post about a month later, made a statement that Zimmerman was let go because there was no way they could disprove his claim that he had acted in self-defense.

He said that under Florida's 'stand your ground' defense, the police were prohibited from making an arrest, and that Zimmerman had the right to defend himself using lethal force.

News of the shooting spread, along with the fact that here was a "white Hispanic" who had killed an unarmed black teenager who was simply walking home from the convenience store with his Skittles. No charges were filed.

Protests began. The national media, again, took to the airwaves to report that racial injustice was once again afoot in the nation.

So, six weeks after the shooting, a special prosecutor appointed by Florida Governor Rick Scott, charged Zimmerman with murder. The case would be played out in the courts.

And boy was it ever.

And then came the feds. The Department of Justice announced its own investigation and the FBI also said they would investigate to see if Martin's civil rights were violated.

The Sanford Police Department's chief investigator, Chris Serino, told the FBI that he believed that Zimmerman's actions were not racially based, but rather based on Martin's attire, a dark colored hoodie, and the unique circumstances of the encounter including the previous criminal activity in the neighborhood. (see the chapter herein on 'thug mentality').

The autopsy report determined that Martin had been killed from a shot from 1-18 inches away, this consistent with Zimmerman's account of the facts and the struggle initiated by Martin.

Plus, the only eye-witness stated that he saw Martin on top of Zimmerman while Zimmerman was yelling for someone to help him.

Zimmerman's account of the actual moment of the confrontation, which were given in an interview to Sean Hannity of Fox News, on July 18, 2012, were that he had gotten out of his truck to see if he could find an address to where Martin had gone.

As he was walking back to his truck in the backyard of some of the residences on the sidewalks, Martin suddenly appeared, "out of nowhere," "from the darkness," and "jumping out of the bushes."

Zimmerman said that Martin asked him, "You got a fucking problem homie?" Zimmerman indicated that he replied no and Martin said, "You got a problem now," and punched Zimmerman. They went to the ground with Martin on top pounding Zimmerman's head into the concrete.

Zimmerman says he yelled for help numerous time with Martin still on top, punching him.

Then, according to Zimmerman, when Martin saw that Zimmerman had a gun he reached for it and said, "You're going to die tonight motherfucker."

Zimmerman says he reached the gun first and shot Martin.

If you believe Zimmerman's story and obviously the jury did, it appears that Trayvon Martin was emulating to be a thug. (again, see the chapter on 'thug mentality') From his age, to his dress, to his demeanor, to his language, to his actions of attempting to attack the neighborhood watchmen, he was a 'thug' through and through.

So for CNN and most other media, acting just like they were supposed to according to my notion of a politically-correct mindset of reverse discrimination, to show only those photographs mentioned earlier of Trayvon Martin as a smiling baby-faced black teenager (they did, go look em up) and Goerge Zimmerman from a much earlier mug shot, is totally misleading, or, depending on how you want to look at it, totally leading, towards a conclusion that another racial injustice had been committed in society.

Even NBC had misrepresented, or made an editing error, as to one aspect of Zimmerman's statements made to 911, which they later corrected.

Apparently NBC reported that Zimmerman had VOLUNTEERED the race of Martin to the 911 dispatcher, when in fact the dispatcher had actually asked Zimmerman what Martin's race was.

Probably the worst part of the whole Trayvon Martin/George Zimmerman case though, and which, again goes to prove the existence of my politically-correct mindset of reverse discrimination more than anything is CNN's creation, or at least overuse, of the term "White Hispanic" in describing George Zimmerman.

They had to though, in order for the story to even be about race, (and remember again, some of the jurors and all of the court personnel involved said race was never a factor) so they could lead the shouts out across America, with the support of blacks and all the race- baiters, that another case of grave racial injustice had occurred.

A white (Hispanic) man had killed an unarmed black teenager.

And the mindset..................... grew!

Chapter 22: Michael Brown, Eric Garner and Dillon Taylor

Those names ring a bell?

Right?

Sure. We all know those people.

Well, maybe kinda?

For one, we all know who Michael Brown and Eric Garner were, even if you've only kept up slightly on the national news recently through television, the internet, or newspapers.

And you definitely know who the first two were even if you only occasionally watch CNN. Goodness knows those two and their stories have been plastered all over CNN for the last several months.

But who is the third name listed?

Dillon Taylor? Hmmm. Who is that?

You haven't seen his name, face, picture or story on CNN or very little, if any, other media, have you?

So who is that?

Dillon Taylor was shot in the parking lot of a 7-Eleven in Salt Lake City on August 11, 2014 by a cop. He was unarmed. The police office was cleared in the death because he thought the young man was armed, though no weapon was found.

Well that's just like, or similar to the deaths of Michael Brown and Eric Garner, right? Brown was shot by a cop. Garner died after a choke-hold was put on him by a policeman.

So we all should know who Dillon Taylor is, and his name should be just as familiar to us as Michael Brown and Eric Garner.

His story, you would think, in happening during the same time frame as the two other deaths would have been all over the likes of CNN, Fox, and all other major newspapers and media. Right?

But it wasn't. So why?

Plain and simply, because Dillon Taylor was WHITE and his killer was a cop who was a BLACK!

This clear double standard in the totally polar opposite manners in which these three deaths were covered, or not, by the media clearly shows and proves the existence of a politically-correct mindset of reverse discrimination, and furthers my notion of excessive black pandering.

If blacks are killed by whites, and especially white cops, we hear about it. If whites are killed by blacks or black cops, we don't.

Michael Brown and Eric Garner were unarmed black men who were killed by white police officers and the stories of their deaths is all the people of America saw on their television sets, heard on their radios, or saw and/or heard on their internet surfing devices for almost all of the fall and winter of 2014.

Al Sharpton and his gang were all over the top of those stories. Americans sat on the edge of their collective seats as they awaited the results of grand juries convened to look into these deaths.

And once the verdicts were released, which exonerated the white officers involved in the deaths, look out.

Then came the protests, marches, violence. You name it.

But what about the death of Dillon Taylor?

Nothing. Al Sharpton wasn't there. Jesse Jackson wasn't there. Nor were there television cameras and reporters.

Nothing. Because he was WHITE!

Further, the Salt Lake City local media, where Dillon Taylor was killed, even down-played the color of the officer, calling him simply, "non-white." If you remember, the very first thing we all heard about in the killings of Brown and Garner, was that WHITE cops had killed BLACK unarmed men.

Also, do you remember shortly after the Garner grand jury released their non-indictment we all heard a separate story that a man had killed two cops in Brooklyn.

Go back and look at the media. Go back and read the stories.

There was absolutely nothing in the early stages of the reporting (I know because I was desperately trying to find out in preparation for another writing session on this book!) and even little in subsequent reporting, that the killer was black, and that the cops were not black.

To be fair, officers Wenjian Liu and Rafel Ramos, who were the cops shot on December 23, 2014 were asian and hispanic, respectively. Not necessarily white, even though they looked more white than black, but they were definitely NOT black.

The killer, Ismaaiyl Brinsley was reportedly a muslim, but clearly a black one.

The point being that we heard nothing about the black versus white makeup of these individuals, even though Brinsley's instagram page left extensive references that the killings were to be payback for the Garner and Brown killings.

The media ignored and failed to mention any racial implications instead giving it the angle that it was a vendetta against law enforcement.

And what about Megan Boken? You probably didn't hear that name either.

She was a white former Saint Louis University volleyball player killed by two black teenagers in St. Louis on August 18, 2012. The two were charged with her murder.

Its kind off odd, but go back and read ABC News coverage online of the murder.

Nowhere, nowhere, is it mentioned that Boken was white and the two killers were black. But we all know what and how it would have been reported had the races of the participants been reversed.

And what about Antonio West, the 13 month old white baby boy shot dead in his stroller by two black teens in Brunswick, Georgia?

Didn't hear much about that one either, did ya?

But you can bet your bottom dollar that if that baby had been black and the shooters white, it would have been all over the media, and perhaps that black baby would today be the poster child of a new civil rights movement!

Chris Lane? He was a white college baseball player shot in Oklahoma in August of 2013 by a black teenager who stated he, "wanted to see someone die."

Terrible, but you probably didn't hear about it because Chris was white, his killer was black. Reverse the races?

Mayhem.

Brian Epp? Daniel Adkins? Christopher Cervini?

I figure you haven't heard of them either, or at least till I mentioned them in an earlier chapter.

Brian Epp was a white construction worker who was killed by a black man by the name of John McNeil in Cobb County, Georgia on December 6, 2005. I bet you never heard anything about Epp's death.

The facts were very similar to the Trayvon Martin death except the races of the parties were reversed. Epps apparently approached McNeil with a box cutter. McNeil shot him. He claimed self defense.

McNeil was originally not charged with the crime but was charged later. He ended up pleading to manslaughter, got sentenced to life but ended up serving about 6 years.

To remind you, Cobb County, Georgia, where the shooting of Epp occurred, is only about 6 hours and one state away by car from Sanford Florida, where the death of Trayvon Martin occurred, even less by plane. But the two places, again, are a million miles apart as far as the racial treatment of the two cases by the media and the collective racial consciousness of society.

Why?

Because of the politically-correct mindset of reverse discrimination.

When blacks are killed by whites, it's a racial media circus. Lights, camera, action! Cue CNN. Cue first guest Al Sharpton.

When whites are killed by blacks?

Nothing.

Daniel Adkins was a 29 year old mentally disabled man killed in Arizona by a black man around the time of the Trayvon Martin/George Zimmerman jury trial. His facts were eerily similar to the Trayvon Martin case in that the black man was claiming self defense, just like Zimmerman. Again, I am pretty sure you never heard of Daniel Adkins.

As close as the Brian Epp and Daniel Adkin deaths were to Trayvon Martins, it doesn't hold a candle to the similarities, aside from the race reversal of course, of the death of Christopher Cervini. He was a 17 year old skinny teenager who was shot and killed by a 42 year old BLACK neighborhood watchman by the name of Roderick Scott on April 4, 2009 in Greece, New York, just outside of Rochester.

Scott was charged with murder but was acquitted under New York's self defense law.

And even though the facts of this case were almost similar to the Trayvon Martin/George Zimmerman case (Trayvon Martin's death occurred on February 26, 2012) I would wager a bank that 90 percent of the people reading this heard nothing of this case in New York.

No major media coverage. Nothing.

You would at least think, as discussed in an earlier chapter, that during the coverage of the later death of Trayvon Martin there would have been a mention of the Cervini death and case, if for no other reason than the similarities of facts and the fact that both cases seemed to hang on interpretations of each state's self defense laws, and the subsequent national uproar to amend the broadness of self defense protections, and particularly the "stand your ground' laws of self defense that were in effect in Florida, and other states, at the time of the Trayvon Martin/George Zimmerman trial.

I hate to stress the point again, but it would actually have made good news to compare the defenses in the two states and the various other states.

In New York the standard was that deadly force was justified if a person felt that it was necessary because he reasonably believed that deadly force was being, or was about to be used against him. But only after a showing that retreat was not an option.

In Florida self defense was covered under the 'stand your ground' defense, which is similar, but slightly different from the New York standard, in that 'stand your ground' does not include an element of retreat.

It makes perfect sense that in an "equal' world (and I mean racially equal here) both cases would have been talked about to compare the laws applicable to each.

It simply would have made for good journalism to have a story talking about and comparing the two cases.

. But hey, because of the politically-correct mindset of reverse discrimination which exists in our society and the excessive pandering of blacks, we were only allowed to hear about the case where a white person, or should I say white hispanic person killed a black person (Trayvon Martin/ George Zimmerman), or where a white cop had shot and killed a black teen (Michael Brown), or where a white cop had choked a black man who later died (Eric Garner), and not about the countless other cases where blacks killed whites.

Dillon Taylor, Megan Boker, Antonio West, Chris Lane, Brian Epp, Daniel Adkins, Christopher Cervini?

You didn't know who they were, did you?

You do now!

Chapter 23: Ferguson

As I begin this chapter, it's currently January 17, 2015 and I am sitting in a room in the Bywater section of New Orleans, one of the most diverse cities in America, and one of my favorites.

I decided to write this chapter on Ferguson and my first point of research (isn't Google amazing?) was the CBS News website.

Now, I have dogged CNN continually in this book about what I feel is their totally one-sided coverage of just about anything to do with race, as in always taking the black, or here, the Michael Brown was murdered and charges should be filed viewpoint.

So in going to CBS I was kind of thinking it might be a more unbiased take on things?

Boy was I ever wrong!

The pandering of blacks was not just excessive and excessive to CNN, it was widespread as well.

CBS had an entire page devoted to Ferguson, with links to other pages.

To my surprise, it appeared that all of the stories were from the black viewpoint, or the side that was in favor of an indictment of Officer Darren Wilson for the shooting of Michael Brown.

The story on the top left of the page (there were two columns) was headlined, "NAACP seeks new grand jury in Ferguson police shooting. The next one under that was headlined, "Ferguson grand juror sues St. Louis County Prosecutor."

An accessible video further down was about the Department of Justice continuing the probe into the shooting of Brown. Another video was of the President of the NAACP calling the grand jury verdict, "Salt in the wound of a brutal injustice."

Several other stories were about all of the "hands up, don't shoot" protests from various places across the country. Yet another story was titled, "Poll: Race relations in the U.S. at new low."

One story was about a bar in Missouri which had apologized for offering a Michael Brown special, which was six shots for a discounted price, the number being a reference to the number of times Brown was shot.

In fact, of the 36 stories or videos on the CBS News web page, only two, yes two, seemed to have been written from the white, or Darren Wilson was justified, viewpoint.

One story was about the Berkeley, California mayor calling certain protesters there, "cowards and thugs." The other story, which was at the very bottom of the page, talked about how the anti-police violence protests in California had turned violent.

A few of the stories on the web page seemed neutral.

I saw no stories which directly appeared to support the verdict.

None.

And if you remember, the grand jury was allowed to look at all of the evidence, backward and forward over a period of several months.

They looked at the results of three different autopsies done on Michael Brown. They listened to various experts in shooting reconstruction and from many other fields, heard testimony from any and all of even the people who claimed to be witnesses to the shooting itself or something to do with the shooting.

Black Pandering

I listened to St. Louis County Prosecutor Bob McCullough, and felt he did a better than average job of explaining the reasons for no indictment.

The grand jury was comprised of 12 members. Nine were white, three were black.

And many of you may not know, but those grand jury members had been picked for that grand jury even before Michael Brown was shot, meaning they had not been picked JUST for the Michael Brown grand jury.

The makeup of the grand jury was based on the population percentages of St. Louis County, in which Ferguson was located. (the population of the city of Ferguson, itself, at the time, however, was about 85 percent black.)

I, for one, had made statements to my circle of friends and family and business associates that I could trust the grand jury's judgment, meaning that if they had chosen to indict Darren Wilson, then I could accept, that having looked at all of the evidence, they had made the right call.

So why couldn't blacks look at it that way?

There was absolutely no way they were going to do that. Everyone saw that.

And that is why the media got all geared up and came to Missouri in droves, why Missouri Governor Jay Nixon called up the National Guard, and why the police braced themselves and planned for how to combat protests.

I wonder what the blacks would have done had there been an indictment. I doubt even that would have made them happy.

Look more at the facts.

Michael Brown was, in my opinion, a thug. (See the chapter herein on 'thug mentality')

It's pretty clear he had bitch-slapped a store owner a few minutes prior to the shooting. And from all of the evidence of the grand jury and the witnesses, he clearly assaulted Officer Wilson.

In other words, he had just committed two crimes which were felonies in Missouri and would have been felonies in any state in the country.

But all we heard about from day one was, "white cop shoots unarmed black teenager."

How about a little, "black teenager attacks white cop and gets shot?"

Goodness knows that when the two police officers where shot a short time later in Brooklyn, in December of 2015, we didn't hear that a black Muslim had shot two non-black cops, did we?

It was generic.

The races of those involved in that shooting weren't even mentioned, at least for several days. All we heard was that two policemen had been shot. It took me a day or two of actual research (that sounds better than two days of Googling) to even determine the races involved in the Brooklyn shooting.

So why?

Black pandering?

For one, I feel like the media coverage was biased in favor of blacks right from the night of the shooting of Michael Brown, on August 9, 2015.

"White cop shoots unarmed black teenager," was all America heard.

Protests and violence began on the second night after a candlelight vigil for Brown. But it seemed that the violence associated with the protests were minimized by the media.

Black Pandering

Instead, most of what we heard were reports about the police response in Ferguson.

People began looting and as many as 11 businesses were looted and vandalized, including a Quik Trip convenience store which was burned to the ground.

But all that the nation seemed to hear on the national media was how the police used tear gas, rubber bullets, riot gear and helicopters to combat the violence.

Well what were the police supposed to do?

Now the tone of reporting probably wasn't helped out by the fact that some reporters got too close to the protesting and ended up getting arrested themselves, including Wesley Lowery of the Washington Post and Ryan Rielley of the Huffington Post.

Oops.

And reporters from Al Jazeera were reportedly shot with rubber bullets and tear-gassed, and their equipment was dismantled.

Oops again.

This didn't help a story already slanted away from the protests and against, or toward the police.

Martin Baron, executive editor of the Washington Post stated that police behavior was, "wholly unwarranted and an assault on the freedom of the press to cover the news."

And from there the reporting got even worse, or more one-sided, depending on your point of view. CNN devoted coverage to an officer telling protestors, "Bring it, you fucking animals, bring it."

It was reported that Missouri Senator Claire McCaskill, D-MO, once a prosecutor for Jackson County, Missouri, said, "the militarization of the police escalated the protestors' response."

Missouri Governor Jay Nixon, also a former prosecutor in Missouri, directed the Missouri State Highway Patrol to take over the policing duties in Ferguson, and urged them to, "back off a little bit."

Even President Obama criticized the police response, "There's also no excuse for police to use excessive force…. against peaceful protestors…."

I guess a good question to ask is—how were the police supposed to act in the face of all the violence that was Ferguson?

Looting, fires being started everywhere, businesses and property vandalized?

Unfortunately, it was the police response that got the media's attention and not the violence.

In fact, in USA Today from December 2, 2014, St. Louis Alderman Antonio French commented, "A lot of folks feel like the only way they can get heard or get a reaction is through setting things on fire and tearing things up….."

Does that sound like an attempt to excuse the violence perhaps?

French further indicated, according to USA Today, that the varied reactions to the grand jury's decision illustrate the complexities in the life stories of African Americans in the St. Louis region who feel powerless to force change.

Yep. An excuse for the violence.

For all that slavery I suppose.

Black Pandering

Ferguson resident Anthony Reliford, said the world shouldn't be surprised to see the residents burning local businesses because local residents don't reap the economic benefit. Wealthy people and police hold the power, he said, also according to the article in USA Today, which was written by Yamiche Alcindor.

What kind of logic is that?

That's like me saying I don't reap the benefits of Disney World, so I might as well go burn it down. (Please don't let that get me on some sort of list. It was only an analogy!)

The article also quoted the Rev. Osagyefo Sekou who said, "You didn't just see buildings burning, you saw democracy on fire," adding further that the grand jury decision convinced some people that peaceful protests don't necessarily bring justice. "It was pain on display," he said.

Again, an excuse for the violence, or so it seems.

So how could these citizens of the St. Louis area and most of the media, have gotten to the point of excusing all of the fires, looting and violence that was Ferguson?

They are victims of my politically-correct mindset of reverse discrimination might be the answer. And that blacks in today's society are pandered to anytime there is a cry of racism, might be another answer.

To say the least, Ferguson was a mess, and very likely my notion of a politically-correct mindset of reverse discrimination being played out, along with some possible blunders by the police along the way, resulted in the very one-sided coverage out of Ferguson. Except for Fox.

Here was yet another case being presented by the national media, primarily from the black viewpoint—that an unarmed black teenager had been shot by a white cop.

Which causes me to bring up the question of how can our society be so skewed that media coverage is different for cases where blacks get shot by whites versus the other way around?

In another chapter I chronicled several instances where whites had been shot or killed by black and black cops, where there was NO national coverage at all!

None.

Our collective society as a whole heard nothing about those shootings, and nothing about the racial overtones that those shootings clearly seemed to have.

And then when the grand jury verdict, or decision, arrived, everywhere, from every angle came nothing but the suggestion, the assumption, that the verdict was wrong.

The police department of Ferguson, which was almost all white (50 of 53 officers were indeed white), in a city that was 85 percent black, through Officer Darren Wilson, had racially profiled unarmed black teenager Michael Brown and gunned him down out of discrimination.

And then a grand jury had railroaded the decision in favor of Officer Wilson.

But after the verdict, (It was not actually a verdict, but a decision to not indict) and maybe because of the state of things prior to and leading up to the verdict, explained above, the Ferguson story just got bigger and bigger.

And the truly bad part is that the media, and even worse, our society, with its politically-correct mindset of reverse discrimination, allowed it to get bigger and bigger and bigger.

The pandering grew.

Black Pandering

It was allowed for everyone, everywhere, to assume there must have been discrimination of white against black in Ferguson.

The grand jury's decision wasn't enough.

Protests erupted in as many as 170 cities across the nation, as most media outlets criticized the process for failing to return an indictment.

Violence occurred in several, along with looting, but we didn't see much of that on TV.

Amnesty International shortly thereafter posted a form letter and requested it be printed, signed and sent to Governor Jay Nixon of Missouri, the head of the Missouri Highway Patrol and various other law enforcement officials in Missouri. In the letter it cited that, "the response from law enforcement to the protests undermined the rights of individuals to peaceful protest,"

The group had even sent a team of human rights 'observers' to Ferguson, the first time in its history that it had ever done such a thing. In a report released in October of 2014, they declared human rights violations in Ferguson.

Imagine that?

Obviously, there was not near as much support for the law enforcement, or officer Darren Wilson's viewpoint, even after total chaos and violence and some 20-25 fires which may or may not have been in response to Michael Brown's step father, Louis Head who shouted to a throng of protestors shortly after the verdict, "Burn this bitch down."

I remember several segments on CNN with various guests and psychologists, even the president of the NAACP, (his words are discussed later in this chapter) down-playing the words as just an emotional outburst after a very emotional moment.

Tiddlywinks! (Because I am not sure if it's appropriate to call it bullshit!)

Inciting a riot comes closer to describing those words!

Further, there was a long string of stories which attacked the previous law enforcement experience of Officer Wilson, with such titles as, "Darren Wilson was Low Profile Officer with Unsettled Early Days." Or how about, "Ferguson Officer's First Job was on Police Force Disbanded Amid Racial Tensions and Probe." Or, "Amid Conflicting Accounts, Trusting Darren Wilson."

An interesting note is that on the first and second night of protests, (or riots as the case may be) CNN's reporters were literally and physically located on the side of the protesting/rioting blacks, while Fox's reporters were literally and physically located on the side with the police.

The Washington Times reported that a symbolic grand jury, "The Black People's Grand Jury" made up of black leaders in St. Louis looked at evidence for two days (the actual St Louis grand jury which returned a non-indictment of officer Wilson took three months to look at all of the evidence) and voted 11-1 to indict officer Wilson on charges of first degree murder, which got reported on the CBS St. Louis affiliate.

Said a member, which was also reported, "Black people… cannot trust our children, the future of our community, in the hands of this establishment, that has proven to us over and over again its disregard for black life."

Now I question why was such a sham event even reported. How is that news?

Answer?

It's only news, given the mindset of our society which panders to blacks, which allows the assumption that blacks are discriminated against by whites.

The NAACP's Legal Defense and Educational Fund actually did send a letter to St. louis County Circuit Judge Maura McShane requesting a new grand jury be reconvened to look again at the shooting of Michael Brown, citing, "grave concerns," and asking for a special prosecutor, alleging that

St. Louis Prosecutor Bob McCullough gave preferential treatment to officer Wilson. (Of course McCullough is white)

The Department of Justice chimed in and announced their own and separate investigation into the death of Michael Brown and into the practices of the Ferguson Police Department and later concerning the death of Eric Garner in Staten Island, New York.

Some 40, yes 40, FBI officers were sent door to door to look for potential witnesses. Additionally the DOJ confirmed that attorneys with the Civil Rights Division from the United States Attorney's Office were participating in the investigation.

Statements were made by President Obama and Attorney General Holder.

Gosh, why doesn't the Department of Justice go investigate, and President Obama and Attorney General Holder make some statements about the racial implications in the deaths of Dillon Taylor, Megan Boker, Antonio West, Chris Lane, Bian Epp, Danial Adkins, and Christopher Cavini? (discussed in an earlier chapter, these deaths of whites shot by blacks or black cops are discussed at length)

Who, you ask?

Exactly.

The Department of Justice will never launch separate investigations into these tragic deaths, but in a truly equally racial world, where blacks weren't so pandered to, they would.

POLITICO recently ran an article that hailed Ferguson as the "New Civil Rights Movement."

So does that make Michael Brown the poster boy of this new movement?

Seriously?

Gotta be kidding me.

Go watch the movie 'Selma' which came out in January, 2015. It is the story of the events that unfolded around the time of the Dr. Martin Luther King, JR-led march across the Edmund Pettus Bridge (a side note, which you might not have known, and somewhat ironic, is that Edmund Pettus was a confederate soldier and later Grand Dragon of the Ku Klux Klan) in Selma, Alabama, in 1965, concerning the rights of negroes to vote in that state after the passage of the Civil Rights Act of 1964.

The movie shows how protesting can be done with class.

We never saw MLK loot a store for a pair of Nikes, wait, it was the 1960's, Converse tennis shoes, or Rosa Parks rob a solon for the latest hair goo.

I have long been a fan of the non-violent works of MLK.

You probably would not have guessed that would you? But yeah, he and his fellow blacks, to be able to protest non-violently in that day and age was amazing. And to have accomplished as much as they did? Nothing but admiration from me.

And most importantly when comparing their efforts and accomplishments to today's civil right 'leaders,' they did it with class. Tough to believe.

But things were clearly different then, if you would-be protestors of today would take heed. Blacks were fighting for basic everyday human rights, like being able to sit anywhere anyone else could on a bus, or to eat in the same restaurant as everyone else, and the basic right to vote. In short, for basic human dignity.

So to take an event like Ferguson and declare it to be the birth of a "New Civil Rights Movement' and to annoint a criminal, a thug, such as Michael Brown the poster boy of the new movement is ridiculous, to say the least.

I think MLK would have rolled over in his grave as Michael Brown's step father Louis Head jumped to the podium, a grown man with his pants halfway down his ass showing his underwear, and angrily and vehemently screamed, "burn this bitch down, burn this bitch down" over and over and over again.

That's the one moment about all of the Ferguson story that many, and probably most whites, the silent white majority, if you will, will see as THE take away moment from Ferguson.

Here was a thug being a thug, protesting over the death of a felony-committing thug, and his rants were nothing but violent and hateful. "Burn this bitch down."

And burn it did. Maybe some protestors were peaceful, maybe even most. But it's hard to ignore the rants of Head, and the fires that ensued.

But the national media, except for Fox, downplayed the rants of Head, and the aftermath of violence and fires.

CNN tried for a week or more to dismiss Head's rants as causing the violence and fires and even had Cornell Brooks, president of the NAACP to come on Erin Burnett's Out Front program and attempt to soothe the potential damage that Head's rants might cause to the "New Civil Rights Movement."

Brooks specifically stated that, "I don't think that was a call for violence, or that it caused violence." And after Burnett reminded him that Head, "had to be in a lot of pain" Brooks went on a lengthy discussion excusing the alleged call for violence as insignificant to the entire debate about the events in Ferguson.

And alas, because of this entrenched mindset of reverse discrimination, this pervasive notion that we are always going to assume that blacks are the victims of discrimination by whites wherever there is a question, almost all of our national media, again except for Fox, continued to promote and spoon-feed the nation that the Ferguson grand jury decision was wrong, and that poor Michael Brown was a victim of racial discrimination.

And like throwing gas on a fire (pun not intended) helped along by the non-indictment of officer Daniel Pantaleo in the choke-hold death of Eric Garner (which I feel was a wrong decision, by the way) the media kept hammering away.

Pandering and more pandering.

In fact, according to a poll of editors and news directors conducted by the Associated Press, the killing of unarmed blacks by police (including Ferguson and the death of Michael Brown) was the number one news story of 2014.

And my politically-correct mindset of reverse discrimination just continued to get worse and worse, and rooted itself even more into the fabric of American life.

And the fires of Ferguson still burn!

Chapter 24: "Nigger"

That's the word used several years ago by celebrity chef Paula Deen, a white person, who admitted to the use of the word in a deposition she had given some time ago. The result of her admission for using the word was a loss of approximately $12 million and the backing of sponsors such as Sears, J.C. Penny, and Walgreens as well as being yanked from her cooking show on the Food Network.

Essentially, she suffered the potential loss of her entire career.

"Nigga, Nigga, Nigga"

"nigga, niggas, nigga, nigga, nigga, nigga, nigga, nigga, nigga, nigga, nigga, nlgga, nigga, N I G G A, nigga,"

The same word, or rather version thereof which should mean the same if we truly lived in a world of racial equality, as used that many times in the Gansta Rap song "Nigga Nigga Nigga" from the album Glockumentary, released in 2008.

There were no losses of careers or sponsors here. In fact, the album containing this song is listed on several lists as one of the most popular albums of the gangsta rap genre, and whose copies on YouTube have been viewed millions, yes millions, of times.

This song also contained such racially derogatory statements if said by a white person, that is (i.e. Fuzzy Zoeller, discussed later in this chapter) as, "nigga, nigga, nigga, nigga, nigga, nigga, nigga, why you eat so much chicken?" and "nigga, nigga, nigga, nigga, nigga, nigga, nigga, cause them hoes is bitches!"

So why is there such a difference?

Why can blacks use the word at will, and even in derogatory contexts, but whites dare not mention the word for fear of society's repercussions?

Pandering to blacks?

Many celebrities and professional athletes, etc have either had careers ruined or nearly so for mere mentioning the word, or using versions thereof, or making racial comments.

Not so with blacks. The word is rampant in the rap music genre. And it seems the nastier the context in which the word is used and the more times its used, the more popular the song and singer become.

Black comedians call each other 'nigger' all the time. Arsenio Hall made a living out of doing it. Chris Rock. Others.

Hardly equality here, is there?

Again, it's the politically correct mindset of reverse discrimination. If whites use the word, its presumed discriminatory. But almost any use of the word by blacks is accepted.

In his song, "Straight Up Nigger" Ice T raps, "I'm a nigga in America. And that much I flaunt," and in fact a large part of his sales are to white America.

In the recent movie, "Trespass" a movie about inner-city rappers portraying gang members on a treasure hunt, they call each other "nigger" more than they use each other's names.

And every Friday night on Home Box Office 'Russell Simmons' Def Comedy Jam features cutting edge black comedians who frequently use the word, "nigger." One veteran stand up black comedian, Paul Mooney, features routines with such titles as, "Nigger Vampire" "1-900-Blame a Nigger" "Niggerstein" and "History Nigger."

Other rap songs or names of groups which use the word 'Nigga,' and I invite you to go listen to some for yourself are—Snoop Dogg's "For all my Niggaz and Bitches" Jay-Z's "Jigga that Nigga" Notorius B.I.G.'s song "The Realest Niggaz" A Tribe Called Quest's "Suck a Nigga" and there's the group named Niggaz Wit Attitude. Ol' Dirty Bastard uses the word 76 times in his Nigga Please album.

The word is of widespread use in America's gang culture and even the members of one Hispanic gang in Houston Texas refer to each other as 'niggahs."

There are even countless articles which try to explain why it is acceptable for blacks to use the word 'nigger' but that it is never acceptable for whites to do so.

The arguments blacks make for using the word is that it has become a word of endearment among blacks and therefore part of the black culture.

Further, that by using it commonly, it dulls the edginess of the word and strips the word of its ability to hurt.

One great big cop-out maybe?

I think so.

Why, even take a look at how Dictionary.com defines the word—Nigga is used mainly among African Americans but also among other minorities and ethnicities in a neutral or familiar way and as a friendly term of address. It is also common in rap music. However, nigga is taken to be extremely offensive when used by outsiders. Many people consider the word to be as equally offensive as nigger. The words nigger and nigga are pronounced alike in different dialects, and so it has been claimed they are one and the same word.

Well thanks for at least saying the words are the same!

Imagine that.

Our politically-correct mindset of reverse discrimination is so alive and well in the use of the word, 'nigger' and/or 'nigga' that society has even allowed definitions to include the double standard of usage, that it's acceptable for blacks to use it, but not for whites, that there are different meanings to the word, depending on the color of the skin surrounding the mouth that spits it out!

The allowing of different definitions is codified!

Now what is kind of cute, but true and perhaps proves my point about the acceptance of the word, or at least it's 'nigga' form is that in typing this book my HP computer never auto-corrected the 'nigga' spelling of the word!

So who would have ever thought that good old Samuel Clemens (aka Mark Twain) was up to no good when he penned his beloved (at the time) novel in 1885 about The Adventures of Huckleberry Finn, his friend Tom Sawyer and their friendship with a runaway slave named Jim.

I mean, isn't that book just about as Americana as you can get?

Two young boys and their good friend Jim going up and down the Mississippi River enjoying the somewhat mischievous life that young teenage boys do.

Nothing wrong with that, right?

Well, maybe there is. Because that book in its original form as penned by Twain contains the word "nigger" some 215 (yes, count em) times.

And recently the book has become the subject of being either changed to delete the use of the "N" word, or banned entirely from libraries across America.

Of course in today's world if Twain, or his Tom and Huck character had been black themselves, would it have been permissible?

You see, the meaning and usage of the "N" word has changed over the years. And it's because of that changing usage that society today seems to totally struggle with its use or non-use, and what to do or not do, as the case may be, with people who choose to put it out there.

Why even the use of the euphemism, "N word" instead of the actual word, "nigger" has become widely accepted as the phrase one should use to even discuss it.

For further example, some place names historically used the word. Niggerhead Mountain (there was one in California and in Texas), Nigger Hollow, Dead Nigger Creek etc.

In 1967, during those important civil rights years you will note, the United States Board on Geographic Names changed names to use the word Negro instead of Nigger in 143 place names.

Charles G. Ankrom

In 1966, Lady Bird Johnson urged the renaming of the Texas version of Nigger Head Mountain to Colored Mountain.

It's kind of funny but Dead Nigger Creek, also in Texas was renamed Dead Negro Draw. Funny in the fact that the word 'dead' was allowed to remain in the name associated with whatever variety of the "N" word was being used.

Gosh how society has struggled with that word.

To be certain the use of the "N" word has become quite controversial in today's society, since the Civil Rights Era of the 1960's until now.

And it seems to me to have become even more controversial in direct correlation to the growth of this politically-correct mindset of reverse discrimination, and the increase in society's pandering of blacks.

As mentioned earlier, blacks, it seems, can use the word at will.

They claim, again, that the use of the word by and between members of their own race gives them 'power' over the word. At least this was the reason that rap artist Jay Z gave to Oprah Winfrey for the use of the word in his music in an interview in 2011.

And also as indicated earlier, blacks also claim that among their race the use of the word is a term of endearment. And it seems this idea, which society apparently accepts, the rap community has taken and run with.

In addition to the songs mentioned above, everything from Jay Z's "Nigga Please" which contains the word some 19 times, to Notorius Big's "Niggas Bleed, to Kanye West's "Niggas in Paris" All of these, to name just a few, extremely popular.

There is nothing at all about the use of the N word in this type of music being racist.

Nothing!

And many times the context of the usage of the term within the song is clearly derogatory.

Perhaps that should make one wonder how society allows blacks to use the word "nigger" or "nigga" as a term of endearment.

Whites, however, seemingly cannot use the word at all, or make racial references or jokes lest they want to subject themselves the wrath of the media and public, many times losing their jobs or careers.

How can this not be blatant reverse discrimination in its simplest form?

Look at all of the white celebrities, from golf professionals to actors, to talk show hosts, to news reporters, to politcians, who have taken a fall for using the word.

Many have either lost their entire careers or come close to losing them. No category, except perhaps white comedians to some extent is immune.

Look first, way back to 1976, when Secretary of Agriculture Earl Butz, who served in that capacity under Presidents Richard Nixon and Gerald Ford, resigned after being ratted on for telling a racial joke on a commercial plane which included Pat Boone, Sonny Bono, and former White House counsel John Dean after the Republican National Convention in 1976.

Apparently in response to a question from Boone about why the Republican Party could not attract more blacks, Butz responded, "I'll tell you what the coloreds want. It's three things: first a tight pussy; second, loose shoes; and third, a warm place to shit." The scandal it caused almost derailed the Ford presidential campaign of 76.

After his death, in 1998, an online article in Chatterbox called Butz a, "victim of history" and explained how the "gears" of racial progress had tore up Nixon's Secretary of Agriculture. It noted that Butz would be remembered less for his accomplishments as the Secretary of Agriculture under Nixon and Ford than for the racial joke that got him fired.

I suggest maybe the start of my politically-correct mindset?

Could be.

The article indicated, that whereas whites had been previously been allowed to, "tell and laugh at jokes that portrayed black men as lazy, shiftless, and priapic," that by 1976, "whites were learning not to say such things."

And how about the 1988 firing of sports commentator Jimmy 'The Greek' Snyder by CBS for making the statement that blacks were "bred" to be better athletes than whites?

CBS immediately fired Snyder and put out the obvious disclaimer that Snyder's remarks did not reflect the views of CBS Sports.

One brave author, Sam Francis, in his 1993 book, entitled, "Beautiful Losers: Essays on the failure of American Conservatism," wrote, "the practice of ruining a white person once a year in honor of Dr. (Martin Luther) King is becoming a national tradition," in referring to white people who were ruined by the media, blacks, and society for racial remarks.

The book, which was being referred to in an article entitled, "Why do only whites lose jobs over racial remarks?" by Peter Bradley in 2008 in V Dare online, stated that the rate at which whites were being ruined for racial remarks had picked up considerably in the previous 15 years.

My politically-correct mindset growing and growing as I have suggested herein?

Probably so.

Bradley was recognizing in his article the same thing I am questioning here when he said, "A question I have never seen discussed is why only whites seem to suffer the consequences of racial remarks?" He listed many examples, some of which we all remember as being all over the news, and some which were less publicized.

Take Golf Channel broadcaster Kelly Tilghman who was broadcasting the Mercedez-Benz Open in Hawaii in 2008 and made the remark of, "lynch him in a back alley," in response to fellow broadcaster Nick Faldo suggesting, "To take Tiger (Woods) on, well yeah, they should just gang up for awhile until……." She ended up being suspended for two weeks. She made an apology to Woods which he accepted.

But then she and her statement ran into none other than, you guessed, Al Sharpton himself, who pressed the issue. He wanted more than the apology.

He said it didn't matter that Tilghman was a far cry from the likes of Don Imus, who had just lost his job for his, "nappy headed hoes" comment." Sharpton said, "It was the word, not the person or their history that matters….. It is a specific racial term that this woman should be held accountable for….. What she said is racist. Whether she's a racist is immaterial."

All of this, even though Woods by statement said, "We know unequivocally that there was no ill intent in her comments."

In a twist to the Tilghman story, Golfweek magazine ran an article about the incident, featuring a controversial cover portraying a hanging noose. Look it up. The choice of imagery was widely criticized and led to the firing of Golfweek's editor Dave Seanor.

In 1997 pro golfer (yes, golf again, and yes Tiger Woods again) Fuzzy Zoeller found himself in the middle of a 'racist' controversy.

He had finished 34th in a golf tournament, but as the previous year's champion, was commenting about champion Tiger Woods and the next year's champion's dinner, where the previous year's winner picks the menu. ".... You pat him on the back..... and tell him not to serve fried chicken next year.... or collard greens or whatever the hell they serve."

Everyone involved in professional golf knew Zoeller to be one of the top funny men and pranksters, and nicest guys, on the PGA Tour.

That didn't matter.

He was white and he had made a racist comment.

Majors sponsors of his, K-Mart and Dunlop dropped him like a lead balloon. Zoeller made a public apology and a personal one to Woods who accepted it. But the damage was done.

He will forever be remembered by many, not as the top professional golfer which he was, but for the "fried chicken" comment about Tiger Woods.

Yet, Gansta Rap can say "nigga, nigga, nigga, nigga, nigga, nigga, nigga, why you eat so much fried chicken?" and nothing?

Other less famous people who have lost their jobs or careers for racial views or remarks include Mel Bradford, Sam Francis, Chris Brand, Andrew Fraser, Kevin Lamb, and Frank Ellis. Not to mention other more notables such as John Rocker, Paul Hornung, and politician Trent Lott.

Let's take another few examples from the world of sports in which the word 'nigger' or a version thereof was used that all happened during the fall of 2013, but which were treated differently, depending on the color of the person saying it.

First, Philadelphia Eagles wide receiver Riley Cooper, who is white, called a security guard a, "nigger" in July, 2013, at a Kenny Chesney concert.

Second, Richie Incognito, who is white and was a guard for the Miami Dolphins, reportedly called his fellow Dolphin teammate a "half-nigger" a short time later.

Then third, about a week after the Incognito incident, Los Angeles basketball player Matt Barnes, who is black, after a game in which he was ejected for standing up for his teammates tweeted he was, "done standing up for these niggas."

Now, you might think that since we are supposed to be living in a racially equal world, that all three of these incidents, all happening around the same time would all be treated equal right?

Nope. Not even close.

And probably because of this cloud of a politically-correct mindset of reverse discrimination which our society lives under.

For instead of all being condemned, these incidents happening at roughly the same time kicked off a debate about who in our society gets to use the word, "nigger" and who does not.

One writer, Ta-Nehisi Coates, who is black, wrote an article in the New York Times on November 23, 2013 attempting to explain, at least that is what the article seemed to be doing, why it was acceptable for Barnes, who is black, to use the word, but not acceptable for Incognito and Riley, who are white. Barnes, he reasoned, was merely being, "inappropriate" in his use of the word, while Incognito and Riley were being, "violent and offensive."

He concluded his article with these words, ""Nigger" is the border, the signpost that reminds us that the old crimes don't disappear. It tells white people that, for all their guns and all their gold, there will always be places they can never go."

Does this explanation indicate a racially equal world?

Heck no.

Rather, the opposite, a world where blacks have been discriminated against for so long, that society will now pander to them, at least as far as the use of the word, 'nigger' or the making of racial remarks is concerned.

Take Bryant Gumbel, who just prior to the 2006 Olympic Winter games made a statement which is along the same lines (the superiority of black athletes) of Jimmy 'The Greek' Snyder, who lost his job for his statement.

Dismissing the athleticism on display at the Winter Olympics he stated, "Count me among those who don't care about them (the Winter Olympics) and won't watch them.... so try not to laugh when someone says these are the world's greatest athletes, despite a paucity of blacks that makes the Winter Games look like a GOP convention."

Far from losing, or even hurting his career for making such a racist statement, he was awarded a play by play job with the NFL network.

And I hypothesize that until an equality comes about concerning the use of the N word, as well as in other areas (see my later chapter on my call to action) that racism will continue and not get any better.

For I am also hypothesizing that there is nothing worse for the silent white majority than being told over and over again to treat everyone equal, but continually seeing society, poked and prodded along by the media, give preferential (not equal) treatment to blacks as far as racism is concerned.

The excessive pandering of blacks gets old.

Very fast.

For the record, Richie Incognito lost his job with the Dolphins and couldn't get another job on any other team. Riley Cooper did not lose his job with the Philadelphia Eagles, but was fined an undisclosed amount, apologized and spoke about his support for penalties for racial slurs. He tweeted the following to his followers, "I am so ashamed and disgusted with myself, I want to apologize. I have apologized to my coach Jeff Lurie and Howie Roseman and to my teammates. I owe an apology to my fans and to this community. I am so ashamed and there are no excuses. What I did was wrong and I accept all the consequences."

A nice apology you say?

I suggest it sounds very nice, it seems to cover all the bases, as if suggested by a front office of a team you want to continue playing for.

Matt Barnes was fined $25,000 for his use of the word, and apologized, but much of the sports commentary world stood up for his use of the word, 'niggas.'

Charles Barkley, a basketball analyst for several major sports media outlets openly stated he was a black man that used the N word and that he would continue to use the N word, and that Barnes should not have had to issue an apology for his use of the word in referring to his black teammates.

Further he said it was not for White America to dictate what was appropriate and inappropriate.

Michael Wilbon, also a black sports commentator, on ESPN's Pardon The Interruption show, also speaking of the Barnes incident, said he uses "nigga" among friends, and further took issue with the white people in charge essentially deciding the issue for black people, "going so far as to fine a guy for tweeting a word he is otherwise allowed to use."

Otherwise allowed to use?

He actually said that about Barnes' use of the N word?

Yep.

And blacks want racism to end?

Imagine that.

Yet, they continue to promote a different standard for the use of the word, 'nigger' which has recently been labeled the most offensive word in the English language.

It's a word so offensive we are not supposed to even use it when talking about its use, such that society has developed a euphemism, or 'N word' to use in its place. (You will note, for effect, my use of the word, 'nigger' and the euphemism, 'N word' interchangeably herein)

The way I call it, it either needs to be allowed or not, for everyone. Don't feed me this crap that blacks should be allowed to use it as a word of endearment.

In an article in Teaching Intolerance, A Project of the Southern Poverty Law Center, writer Jason Millstein, who is black, said the N word has, "become a popular word of endearment by the descendants of the very people who once had to endure it."

I just don't see how society can allow such a double standard.

Jesse Jackson, one who purports to be at the forefront of the black cause has called for a moratorium on the use of the N word, yet was caught once using the word on a live microphone during a private 'whispered' conversation.

Popular recording artist Kanye West once taunted the whites in an audience, who had paid not a paltry sum to attend his concert, during the chorus of his song 'Gold Digger' by screaming, "White people! This is your one chance to say nigga."

And black artist Ernest Baker, once stated in an article that he, "sometimes felt that white people were getting away with something when they quote lyrics or retweet lyrics with, 'nigga' in them and I wish it didn't happen but I know it does."

But take another look at the opposite side. Television talk show host and radio talk show host Dr. Laura Schlessinger, who is white, on August 10 2010, took a call from a black woman who was married to a white man who was asking how to deal with her husband when he did not take offense to acquaintances' racial comments.

Schlessinger questioned whether the examples given were actually racist and opined that the caller was being too sensitive and told the caller not to, "NAACP me."

Schlessinger further opposed the concept that blacks could use the word, "nigger" and that whites could not, using the word, "nigger" eleven times herself in the discussion.

After the show Schlessinger took herself off the air and issued an apology to Los Angeles Radio People online journalist Don Barrett. Barret questioned whether the apology had been issued simply because she had been 'caught.'

Schlessinger announced she would end her radio show (I wonder whose idea that really was) and indeed did so at the end of 2010.

Thus, her career was essentially halted (she later began broadcasting on Sirius XM) for even suggesting that it was oversensitive for black people to complain about white people using the N word when blacks use the word so frequently themselves.

There are scores and scores of other whites whose careers and wealth were affected by disparaging comments about blacks, either by the use of the N word or other offensive comments.

Just take a look at Marge Shott, the flamboyant and controversial owner of the Cincinnati Reds whose bad mouthing of blacks, and others (Jews, asians, and gays) eventually led to her ouster from ownership of the team.

And how can anyone forget the circus that started during the Spring of 2014, and continued throughout the year which was Donald Sterling, a white man, the owner who lost his Los Angeles Clippers franchise, uttering racist comments on what was supposed to be a private conversation!

A recording from 2013 of a conversation between him and female friend, V. Stiviano, concerning an Instagram posting she had made of herself posing with former basketball great Magic Johnson, who is black, was released in which he told Stiviano, "it bothers me a lot that you want to broadcast that you are associating with black people," adding, "You can sleep with them, you can bring them in. You can do whatever you want, but the little I ask is… don't bring them to my games."

And boy did it hit the fan once the comments were made public.

Clippers players, who were mostly black, almost boycotted a game but instead wore their shirts inside out to obscure any Clipper logos. The next day members of another team, the Miami Heat wore their uniform tops inside out as well.

And Lebron James, perhaps the predominant player in the NBA today stated that, "There's no room for Donald Sterling in the NBA."

After Lebron, other black basketball players and former players piled on. Kobe Bryant, Kareem Abdul-Jabbar, Kevin Johnson, Shaquille O'Neal, and others.

Sterling's proverbial goose was cooked, despite the fact that Sterling had previously been given a lifetime achievement award by the Los Angeles chapter of the NAACP and was due to receive a second one. (It was cancelled, of course.)

Sterling was given a lifetime ban from the NBA, ordered to never again attend an NBA game and fined $2,5 million dollars, the maximum amount possible. Further he was forced to sell the team. Sterling at first had attempted to fight back, but obviously soon realized it was futile.

The mindset of society was against him.

Again, a white man was showing discrimination and racism against blacks.

As such, he was punished more severely than any sports team owner has ever been punished.

And boy how the spectacle played out. Every day, all across the television sets of America, society watched as the white man was crucified for making racial comments.

And what about Don Imus? I have to admit I never liked the guy and felt his stuff was way too over the top.

But he surely waded out way too deep, at least according to the existence of my politically-correct mindset of reverse discrimination, on his radio show in 2007 when he referred to the Rutgers University women's basketball team as a bunch of, "nappy headed hoes."

Now Imus did apologize under the mounting public pressure.

He called his characterization of the team, "thoughtless and stupid" and said he was sorry?

Enough?

Nope.

Who else but Al Sharpton, chimed in on the onslaught against Imus, calling him, "racist" "sexist" and "abominable," and calling for Imus to be fired.

Black columnist Clarence Page of the Chicago Tribune, who had been a frequent guest on Imus' said he would not appear on the show again and stated that he had known shot jocks who had, "lost their job for less."

Sponsors started pulling ads right and left. General Motors, Proctor and Gamble, American Express, and Sprint, along with others.

And in just about a week, eight days to be exact, Imus was fired. Imus did return to broadcasting but his career has never been the same.

Interesting to note is the popular use, and Imus' use of the term, "nappy," in the racial discussion.

Wanna guess where that came from?

Well it didn't come from a white person!

It came from none other than Stokely Carmichael, the Black Power leader of the 1960's who said of blacks, "our noses are broad, our lips are thick, our hair is nappy, we are black and beautiful."

In other speeches he seemed to denigrate the role of the black woman in the civil rights movement, even suggesting that the best role for 'her' in the race for equal rights was, "prone."

I suppose you might get to 'nappy headed hoes' from there.

But in any event, for Carmichael it was part of his popular anti-white, equality by any means, rhetoric, and his use of the term was fine.

For Imus, it was essentially a career-changing if not career-ending mistake.

Double standard?

For sure.

Pandering?

Even surer!

And how about Michael Richards, the beloved Kramer of the very popular 'Seinfeld' television series?

Also a comedian, on one standup comedy occasion, in 2006 he shouted at a group of black hecklers calling them, "nigger" several times and referred to lynchings and the Jim Crow era.

The backlash was so tremendous that Richards appeared on the Late Show with David Letterman and offered up a public apology.

He even called Al Sharpton and Jesse Jackson to apologize. Sharpton refused the apology.

The incident, according to Richards, was a big factor in his retiring from standup comedy within the next year.

Jason Millstein, a black journalist, in an article in Teaching Intolerance, A Project of the Southern Poverty Law Center, called the use of the N word the ultimate insult that has tormented African Americans for generations (obviously as used by whites) but a popular term of endearment," by the descendants (blacks) of the very people who once had to endure it."

The article itself was a call for teachers to be able to teach the use of the N word accordingly.

So now we have courses in the schools that actually teach that blacks can call each other 'nigger' all they want but that whites can never use the word?

More recently, in February of 2014, popular rap artist Nicki Minaj found herself caught up in the middle of the "who can say 'nigger' when?" double standard debate, when she released an album cover with a popular picture of Malcolm X holding a rifle looking out a window with a slogan attached to it that appeared to say, "Lookin ass nigga."

She was criticized by many for dishonoring the civil rights history of Malcolm X.

I suggest she hit the civil rights history of Malcolm X right on the head.

I mean, wasn't Malcolm X, for the most part, always linked to violence during the civil rights movement?

Manaj apologized and changed the album cover immediately.

Perhaps, instead of apologizing, she should have claimed the use of the word was her 'term of endearment' for the controversial civil rights figure.

In response to the criticism, Manaj responded with a statement that hits the story of this chapter right on the head, "The N word causes so much debate in our community, while so-called N word behavior gets praised and worshiped."

Thanks Nicki!

And just recently, an occurrence happened that so utterly proves the existence of a politically-correct mindset of reverse discrimination, and that blacks are pandered to, more than anything else in this entire book.

In early 2015, the University of Oklahoma closed down its on-campus chapter of the Sigma Alpha Epsilom fraternity for some of its members singing a chant which included the N word on a bus ride home from an event. The singing of the chant was caught on video and hit YouTube. The students were expelled, and a national uproar ensued.

Now, that alone isn't the part that proves my mindset more than anything else in this entire book.

The part that does that is that shortly after the incident, rapper Wocka Flocka Flame, who had previously performed concerts for that fraternity and was stating that he was cancelling an April 2015 concert for that fraternity, was interviewed on CNN and said he was, "disgusted and disappointed in the actions of the SAE fraternity (for their use of the N word)…," further indicating that, "Racism is something I will not tolerate."

I am appalled!

I would love to tell you why!

Have you ever heard the lyrics of Wocka Flocka Flame's rap songs?

I googled just ten of his most popular hits, and ALL TEN, yes let me say that again, ALL TEN, contained the word, 'NIGGA' so many times that I lost count. Hundreds of times in just those few songs.

So here is a rapper who uses the word 'NIGGA' to the utmost degree, for fortune and fame, who has the audacity, the balls if you will, to even come onto the national spotlight, and criticize the students of SAE for using the same word in a chant and he calls them DISGUSTING?

And how about the audacity of the media (shame on you again CNN) for even interviewing him in the first place, playing right into and along with my mindset.

If that doesn't prove the existence of the mindset of politically-correct reverse discrimination for you, the reader, then I am afraid that nothing will!

Point proven!

So, as you can see, and especially with this last example of the pot (Wocka Flocka Flame) calling the kettle (OU frat boys) black, this double standard for the use of the most offensive word in the English language is about as ingrained in society as it possibly could be, blacks are pandered to as much as they possibly could be, and it seems likely to never change!

Chapter 25: The 'Thug Mentality' or 'Thug Culture'

I saw a cartoon on the internet some time ago which showed a famous black and white portrait of Dr. Martin Luther King, Jr. in a well-tailored black suit and tie with a slogan that read, "I had a dream, but it did not involve yo pants hanging half way down yo ass."

These were not his actual words of course, (that we know of) they had just been jokingly attributed to him in the cartoon.

I do wonder, though, if he were still alive today, what he might actually have to say to America's blacks, and particularly the ones purporting to engage in a new civil rights movement, about the way they look, act, talk and appear to the rest of society.

Before you read the rest of this chapter, go back and look at some history books or get on the internet and see for yourself what MLK and his followers were wearing.

What did they look like? How did they act?

How were they dressed?

Suits, and ties like the one in the cartoon just mentioned. The women in dresses. They were usually dressed in what midwest people call 'church' clothes. And in most everything that was on the news of that time be it television or newspapers, they were pictured accordingly.

Do you think that just happened? Or maybe could it just have been that they were different than today's blacks?

Different how?

Or was it just part of a plan?

Whatever the reason, being dressed in suits and ties, the women in nice dresses, (look at the famous picture of Rosa Parks on the Montgomery bus) lended all of those early civil rights crusaders an aire of credibility, even an aire of respectability, suggesting that to whoever they were talking to, or wherever they were marching or protesting, they were at least being respectful of society's norms concerning dress.

And if for no other reason than this alone, perhaps they could be deserving of some semblance of respect in return.

I am not saying or even suggesting that being dressed that way made it easy for those pioneers of the civil rights movement.

Easy it wasn't.

And their struggle for basic human dignity, and to be recognized as having some basic rights that we all now take for granted was an uphill battle, to say the least.

But you have to agree that the way they looked, talked and acted probably did play a role in getting past some of the barriers of that tumultuous time.

But how far do you think MLK and his followers would have gotten had they been dressed like the blacks of today and had the 'thug mentality' or 'thug culture' that exists with so many blacks of today?

Remember my description of the Snipes character for my imaginary movie, "Black Men Can't Read?"

Pants hanging half way down his ass, underwear showing, tattoos everywhere, excessive jewelry and bling. Exaggerated corn rows or dreads for hair, maybe a gold tooth or two, and a flat-billed ball cap titled sideways on the head. A "thug" plain and simple.

And right or wrong, I would suggest that this image of blacks is the way that most of the silent white majority see all blacks, this being the image they see most on their television sets or in their newspapers or on their computers.

Now, am I implying that all blacks today look like 'thugs?'

No way. Not at all.

And it's not just the clothing or the way a person dresses that characterizes them as a 'thug.' even though it could be argued that the way a person dresses is a major factor in how they are treated by others and whether that treatment involves a perception of them as 'thugs.' (as in Trayvon Martin and Michael Brown)

But to be fair, one has to include attitude, disposition, upbringing and many other things, including even the language spoken by blacks, along with looks to reach the determination that someone is a 'thug.'

Take Ferguson for instance, and one of the lasting images from those tumultuous times.

How do you thinks whites are going to respond, when blacks of today look and act like Michael Brown's step father Louis Head, as he angrily jumped up on that platform with Michael Brown's mother, right after the grand jury non-indictment, in his tight t-shirt and low hanging pants with his underwear and ass half way showing, and so angrily and vehemently, with clenched fists raised screamed out, "Burn this bitch down" over and over?

Do you think that is something that whites will give credence to, and help lead to the end of racism?

Or you think maybe that might have the opposite effect?

Now he might actually be a nice guy. But to all of America watching their television sets that night, at that moment, he was a 'thug' plain and simple, regardless of how CNN tried over and over to explain it away in their coverage in the days following his rant.

Take Michael Brown himself and even Trayvon Martin on the days they were shot. Both were young teenagers, at a time of their life when they were approaching manhood with the same pressures society places on young male teens, black and white and all races for that matter, to, "be a man."

"Man up" they say.

I have long said that a boy becomes a man the day he stops feeling like he has to prove he's a man.

I propose Brown and Martin were still trying to prove they were "men," trying to EMULATE the idols they looked up to in music, sports, lifestyles and the like.

They were emulating to be 'thugs.'

Trayvon was wearing a hoodie. In and of itself nothing wrong with that. But in the dark, cutting through a place that he possibly shouldn't be?

And then more importantly how did he act when he confronted George Zimmerman?

Did he mildly explain his presence? Or did he attempt to be the 'thug' that George Zimmerman described him as when he attacked Zimmerman?

The jury apparently thought the latter.

Brown actually proved he was emulating to be a' thug' by his actions in attacking the officer and previously bitch-slapping the store owner in the video from just before he died.

And now Brown is the poster boy for the new civil rights movement? What would MLK think of that?

And if these young men's attempts to emulate 'thugs' weren't obvious, perhaps that's due to the mindset of reverse discrimination, which seems to allow society only to looks at these deaths, along the line of unarmed black teenagers killed by a white cop and a white night watchman (although, again, Zimmerman was actually Hispanic).

One article in Daily KOS, for which the author was not listed, published in November of 2014, was titled, "The thuggification of young black victims of white violence: Is thug is the new nigger?"

The article stated that the thuggification of Martin and Brown, and even Oscar Grant, who was killed while handcuffed by a white policeman in Oakland, "was a modern attempt to 3/5ths their value in the world, while the refusal to ever ascribe the thug label to white perpetrators of violence suggests that the word (thug) is gaining an exclusive connotation limited to African Americans." The article ended with the sentence, "Thug is the new nigger."

I'm sure glad he said that and not me!

I do believe there has developed in our society today what I will call a 'thug mentality,' or 'thug culture' which pervades the black community, mainly younger black men, and this mentality, or psyche, if you will, is evident in the way these blacks think, dress, act, and talk and is based on characteristics which include a disrespect for law enforcement and authority, a disrespect for the family, a clear disrespect for whites (and again, this one is fueled by today's media), and a huge disrespect for women and children.

My second belief, and this is the point that I want to be the takeaway from this book, is that the existence of this 'thug mentality' or 'thug culture,' along with the pandering of blacks, could possibly be an insurmountable barrier to ever overcoming racism in America.

Whites are not going to listen to, or positively respond to the likes of, "burn this bitch down" or to a poster boy like Michael Brown.

Is this 'thug mentality' or 'thug culture' widespread you ask?

Yes is the answer.

Look at some of the statistics, which I feel contribute greatly to the mentality of blacks today and particularly black males.

One can argue the 'thug mentality' or 'thug culture' causes the following statistics or that these statistics are what causes the 'thug mentality' or 'thug culture.'

Either way, it doesn't matter.

The statistics are the statistics and probably need to be dealt with if we ever hope this 'thug mentality' or 'thug culture' has a chance of not grabbing ahold of the black males of our society the way it seems to do.

But consider.

Roughly 67 percent of black children are raised in single parent homes and 88 percent of those are in a home with single mothers.

Essentially, the fathers are absent.

Compare that to only 25 percent for single parent white homes.

Further, the percentage of blacks who marry has declined tremendously from 64 percent in 1970 to just 32 percent in 2004.

As far as education is concerned, in 2010 only 52 percent of black males graduated from high school.

By the time students reach the ninth grade 42 percent of black males have been suspended or expelled from school, compared to only 14 percent for white males. The fraction of young men not working or enrolled in school is nearly twice as high for blacks than whites.

Crime? Blacks are incarcerated in America at a rate more than 6 times that of whites.

One simple argument, very simple, but one that may be true, is that black male teenagers, by not being in school or working, have nothing else to do but commit crimes.

Discriminatory statement?

Or my 'thug mentality?'

But why such alarming numbers? And especially as to black men?

A correlation to the black 'thug culture?'

Perhaps.

Maybe it's just not 'manly' for a black man to be saddled with a wife and kids. Perhaps it makes you look 'tougher' if you are alone and not married and have several children by several different 'bitches' or 'hoes.'

And sadly the statistics on that point are higher for blacks than for whites as well.

The Moynihan Report, written about 50 years ago by Assistant Secretary of Labor, Daniel Patrick Moynihan, initiated a debate about whether the African American family structure LEADS to negative outcomes such as poverty, crime, teenage pregnancy and gaps in education, or whether the African American family structure was the RESULT of institutionalized discrimination, poverty, and segregation.

My take again on that point, is it doesn't matter which is correct.

It just needs to be fixed.

But I also think you have to add into the equation the existence of this 'thug mentality' or 'thug culture' and the affect it has had in causing these issues with the African American family structure to continue to get worse and worse over the years.

And I am not alone in this theory.

Ask Bill Cosby, Bill O'Reilly, and others.

Needless to say, society has to address these poverty, crime, teenage pregnancy, and education gaps, and family structure issues of black families in order to ever address racism.

But, unfortunately, I feel this 'thug mentality' or 'thug culture' will have to be addressed first.

You tell me.

I am at a loss.

And if you can come up with the answer to this and get our American society on board about addressing this 'thug mentality' and the characteristics that it includes, then you, my friend, will be a hero.

That could win you a Nobel Prize.

Seriously.

Unfortunately, rather than society looking for ways to change, or do away with, this 'thug mentality,' or 'thug culture' society instead allows it, and even promotes it, or perpetuates it, causing it to grow and grow.

A politically-correct mindset of reverse discrimination maybe?

Pandering to blacks maybe?

Take first the language present in this 'thug mentality' or 'thug culture.'

Blacks of today, and especially urban blacks seem to have their own language.

But don't just take that from me. Look it up.

Let's 'axe' the experts.

Wikipedia defines both the Urban Dictionary AND African American Vernacular English. The latter is also commonly referred to as Black English, Black Vernacular English, and African American English.

Wikipedia calls Urban Dictionary, "a crowdsourced online dictionary of slang words and phrases that was founded in 1999 as a parody of Dictionary.com by then college freshman Aaron Peckham."

As for the African American Vernacular English, Wikipedia called it a. "a variety of American English, most commonly spoken today by urban working-class and largely bi-dialectal middle class African Americans."

How many of you have heard blacks use the word "axe" in place of the word "ask," as in, "Let me axe you a question?" This is just one example.

And sorry but I pulled that one on you a paragraph or two ago!

Widespread?

You decide.

Over one million people go to the Urban Dictionary site every day, and two thousands entries are added daily!

Further, a fact which supports my notion in this chapter of a 'thug mentality' or 'thug culture' is that the Urban Dictionary site's founder, Aaron Peckham indicates that the site is predominantly used by males between the ages of 15-24.

To show some degree of the Urban Dictionary's acceptance in society, consider that the Urban Dictionary was used in a court in Wisconsin in 2013.

In a case involving theft, the dictionary's definition of the word, "jack" as "to steal" was allowed as evidence to lend meaning to two alleged thieves who referred to themselves as, "jack boys."

Even various states Departments of Motor Vehicles refer to the Urban Dictionary in considering if possibly offensive license plate titles are allowed.

For instance, it allowed a license place to say "hoe" when the holder of the plate made claim that it was an Urban Dictionary definition of "tahoe."

It's as if this language has taken on a life of its own. And unfortunately, it's mostly evident right along with the other indicia of this 'thug mentality' or 'thug culture.'

Pandering?

You decide.

There has even been significant controversy as to whether the African American Vernacular English should be taught, or at least allowed to be used by blacks, in the educational system. And the results and opinions on this subject are all across the board.

It even prompted Geneva Smitherman, a noted speaker and authority on the matter to suggest that, "the controversies and debate concerning the African American Vernacular English in public schools implies deeper deterministic attitudes toward the African American community as a whole."

She further describes this as a reflection of, "the power elite's perceived insignificance of, and hence rejection of Afro-American language and culture."

Really? Yet another area where whites are being racist, I guess.

Plus, I wonder if she was taking into account the existence of a Black History Month for African Americans, and everybody else that wants to, to celebrate African American "culture," when the opposite, a White History Month, for whites to celebrate their 'culture' is so glaringly non-existent.

Also, look at the rap and hip hop music of today and the lyrics contained in some of the songs of the biggest artists. Watch a few of the videos.

The lyrics and videos of way too many of these songs out and out promote violence, gangs and gang violence, drugs of course, and treating women like trash. Violence and disrespect against any sort of authority or law enforcement is encouraged.

To black thugs, women, and again, it's usually not your wife, is your "bitch" or your "hoe" and you may have more than one. And very little respect is visible in the way you treat them. The language is horrendous, almost to the point of being vile and evil.

When did this all start?

Hard to say but go back to 1999 and the album with the actual title of, "Thug Mentality" which included a song also named, "Thug Mentality" by rapper Krayzie Bone.

That's as good a place to start as any, though some say rap goes all the way back to the 1980's. The album sold 137,357 copies in its first week and debuted at number four on the Billboard albums rap chart, and it was certified platinum the year it was released.

Here are some of the lyrics from the song, "Thug Mentality" "Niggaz (there's that word again, see the chapter herein) struggle daily, gotta survive…. Niggas let's do in de enemy now, terminate em, eliminate em…. T H U G that's thug, we be T H U G….. Thug we be, that's thug mentality."

Well, maybe it wasn't me that created the "thug mentality" term after all.

That makes it even better!

And by today's standards those lyrics are tame.

From there it got worse and worse and by that I mean more vulgar, more violent, more in your face and the face of authority and society as a whole.

American Statistics shows that among parents with children in school who were surveyed, 47 percent believed that violent messages in rap music contribute 'a great deal' to school violence. Further 66 percent of 13-17 year olds believe that violence in music is partly to blame for violent crime like the shooting at Columbine High School in Colorado in 1999.

Some artists seem to rap ONLY about money, sex, drugs, and alcohol. Some names include Lil Wayne, Eminem (who is white) and Nas.

Many teenagers of today listen to 2-4 hours of rap music per day and seem to be affected by the same. It's as if they attempt to emulate the things they hear and the rappers or hip hoppers they listen to. It's almost as if they can do the same things that the rap songs suggest and be, or become like the rappers themselves.

In an article online entitled, "Worst things about rap music" the following were listed after a statement which comes very close to the subject of this chapter.

It read, "Rap music is amazing in its influence and popularity. Far more than just a musical style, rap and sub-genres of rap have created distinct cultures with specific expectations, status symbols, and norms."

Yep, what I am trying to say exactly!

Some of the things from that list include:

Egotism. Many rap songs can basically be boiled down to "I am the best, toughest, and hardest. Don't agree with me? I will prove it."

Sexism. Since music began, women have been idolized in its lyrics. Not so with rap.

For the most part rap music, unabashedly objectifies women. Instead of being a person you do things with, they become a thing you do stuff to.

From reinforcing a double standard of pimps and hoes, to advocating violence against women (slap a bitch).

Glorification of the gangster mentality. Rappers are claiming to be the gangsters of the world today.

I recall a cartoon on Facebook which showed a picture of some members of one of today's gangs looking strangely similar to my Snipes character from my "Black Men Can't Read" movie, with wife-beater tank tops, low hanging pants and underwear showing of course, tattoos, jewelry or bling, and either flat-billed ball caps or dreadlocks.

Alongside was a picture of some of the actual gangsters of the 1920's with their suits, dress hats and tommy sub-machine guns with a slogan which read, "So you want to be a gangster? Pull up your damn pants!"

One blogger's online blog entitled, "Violence and Rap Music" clearly states that one of the most disturbing aspects of rap music is its violent references to women. It hypothesizes that rappers have changed their perogatives from making music to making money and realize that sex and violence sells.

Rapper Eminem (who in my opinion is a white guy trying to act black) put out the album, "The Marshall Mathers LP" which was one of the fastest selling rap albums in history.

In this record alone, over 75 percent of its content is considered violent and misogynistic, which is defined as, "the hatred or dislike of women,... and can be manifested in numerous ways, including sexual discrimination, denigration of women, violence against women, and sexual objectification of women."

What's more, over 80 percent of his lyrics involved female murders. Out of the 11 songs on the album, nine depict murders of women.

And Eminem is one of the most famous and popular rappers of all time.

As you can see, the case for my 'thug mentality' or 'thug culture' grows stronger and stronger the more you look at our society.

Here's some more of the lyrics from some of today's rap music. I will just present some of it and let you decide what your opinion is.

From the song "Nigga, Nigga, Nigga" by Gangsta Rap. "Yeah, mothafucka... Nigga, Nigga, Nigga, 100 percent Nigga, ... why the police hate Niggas?... I ain't all that African American shit, fuck that, I'm a Nigga, ... why you eat so much chicken? (yes, he said that, I can't or Fuzzy Zoeller can't but he can).... why you call them hoes bitches?.... why your pants gotta sag?"

Rapper 50 Cent appeared on CBS News in 2013 and attempted to refute any connection between his rap music and gun violence, claiming that his music was just a reflection of his experiences and not a glorification of assault weapons.

Here's some of his lyrics from his song "Shooting Guns" "I go to war at my house, stop niggas ain't listening..... I believe you when you say you tough nigga, ... been fucking with the pigs."

Or how about these lyrics, also from 50 Cent, in his rap song, "My Gun Go Off" "Nigga my gun go off..... I'll pop summin....... bullets... go through your ass fast...."

There are even rap songs by black artists specifically promoting violence against whites. Check out these lyrics from the song "Kill Whitey" by Menace Clan, Da Hood, 1995 Rap-A-Lot Records, "Niggas in the church say: kill whitey all night long..... the homies think I'm crazy because I shot a white baby.... I beat a white boy to the motherfucking ground..."

Also in this category is Apache's "Kill d'White People" from the album Apache Ain't Shit, 1993, "Kill the white people, we gonna make them hurt. Kill the white people..."

Once you actually read or listen to some of the lyrics of this stuff, you can easily see how it promotes a 'thug mentality' or 'gang mentality' among the people who buy and listen to it for hours on end, and especially among the blacks, as most of the rappers of today and the past are.

No wonder we hear about shooting episodes and gang and gun violence everyday on the news.

There's also little doubt about the influence of rap music on young people when you consider how immensely popular rap music is among today's genres of music.

Many of the artists listed above are some of the most popular artists in any music category. Jay Z, 50 Cent, Eminem, etc are household names even for people that don't listen to rap!

And do you think there might be some correlation between this 'thug mentality,' or 'thug culture' that has pervaded our society, and the numbers or percentages of blacks who are incarcerated?

I would wager a small house on it.

And to show some timeliness in this rap music theme, did you happen to watch the Grammys on Sunday, February 8, 2015 (that was last night, as I sit and write these few paragraphs) and see this 'thug mentality' shine through from none other than Kanye West?

As just a little background, you might remember back to the 2009 Grammys when Kanye made a 'thug' out of himself, and an 'ass,' at least that's my opinion and one that is probably shared by millions of others, when he stormed onto the stage to interrupt Taylor Swift, who had just won Album of the Year.

He grabbed the microphone and began a 'thuggish' rant on why Beyonce' should have won Album of the Year instead of Swift.

He was criticized extensively in the media for that outburst, enough that most people would think he would have learned his lesson.

But 'thugs' don't.

And he obviously didn't, because Sunday, February 8, 2015, he did it again.

This time it was Beck, who is white, who won Album of the Year, when coincidentally, Beyonce' was once again nominated, and even more coincidentally, Kanye was back to perform on the Grammys. (He hadn't performed or made an appearance for six years since the 2009 fiasco with Swift.)

Dressed in a maroon- colored flannel sweat pant looking outfit, with jewelry and bling and tennis shoes, looking like he had jumped right off a page of 'thug' quarterly, he earlier performed his hit 'One Only' standing over a hole in the stage that seemingly was made to look like a manhole right out of the streets of New York.

He straddled the manhole and groped his crotch a time or two as he 'performed.'

Later, as Beck's win was announced over Beyonce' and others, Kanye again stormed the stage, as he had done to Swift six years earlier, but he appeared to make it look as though he was joking, in that he didn't actually grab the microphone and diss Beck during the show.

After the Grammys, however, in an interview with E!, he made it known that his feelings were real, as he verbally criticized Beck's win over Beyonce,' "I just know that the Grammys, if they want real artists (is he saying black here?) to keep coming back, they need to stop playing with us….." adding that, "…. and Beck needs to respect artistry, and he should have given his award to Beyonce'."

So okay, here we have a grumbling artist, if you want to call him that, making an ass of himself a second time on none other than the Grammys over his perceived opinion of who should have won an award.

But he didn't stop there.

He had to play the race card as he continued his 'thuggish' opinion, "I'm 36 years old and I have 21 Grammys. That's the most Grammys of any 36 year old artist. Out of all those 21 Grammys, I've never won a Grammy against a WHITE artist."

Seriously Kanye? The Grammys are racist?

How many black artists won Grammys that Sunday night?

A lot.

And what's with the insinuation that black artists are better than white ones?

I mean, here's Beck, a man that plays 14 instruments for gosh sakes, who wins an award over a lady that just sings songs written by other song writers?

But Kanye wasn't done. His 'thuggish' rant went on a power trip from there, ".... when Yeezus (his album).... only gets two nominations from the Grammys, what are they trying to prove? Do they think that I wouldn't notice? Do they think that, someway, that I don't have the power to completely diminish all of their credibility at this moment?"

Quite honestly, Kanye, yours was a performance that only a true 'thug' could carry out.

Need more proof that Kanye might be a 'thug?'

Here are some of his lyrics, from his song entitled 'All of the Lights,' which features Rihanna, "All of the lights, Cop lights, flash lights, spot lights. Strobe lights, street lights (all of the lights, all of the lights) Fast life, drug life, THUG life, rock life, every night (all of the lights.)"

Who knows, if Kanye can just get Al Sharpton on board (and I bet that racist comment did the job already) then maybe next year he and Al can host the Black Grammys!

Come on Kanye. Give Grammy viewers a break.

And don't come back for another six years.

And take the maroon flannel sweat pants with ya!

And look at the world of sports. One could easily argue that blacks in some of the major sports that we watch all the time, well..... uh..... look and act like thugs.

NFL and NCAA college football players with their dreadlocks hanging out of their helmets. Many times they are heavily tattooed.

And even their actions in some of the end zone rituals and reactions after plays both good and bad and after penalties clearly can lead one to this impression.

And remember, these folks are supposed to be role models.

And the NBA? The same. As you are probably aware by now, as I have mentioned the NBA several times, most of its players are black.

Uniforms of basketball players cover even less of the body than football uniforms. Because of this, tattoos on many of the players, which cover extremely large portions of their arms and shoulders and are even more easily seen than in football. And consider all of the trash-talking and again, the actions and reactions to fouls and plays, both good and bad.

Even PGA golfer Paul Azinger, who is white and perhaps the farthest thing from a 'thug' there ever was, in 2011 said that NBA superstar Lebron James looked like a thug.

Of course, Azinger was highly criticized, even though I would dare say that many of 'white America' silently agrees with his assessment, perhaps not as to Lebron James specifically, but at least as to many players in the NBA.

Seattle Seahawk defensive back Richard Sherman was also labeled a 'thug' after his loud and proud post-game interview demeanor following the NFC championship game in January, 2014. He said that the word thug was the accepted way of calling someone the N word. (Thug is the new nigger?)

Again, I am glad it's him not me that made that correlation. I watched his interview and it seems the word 'thug' certainly fit.

After the interview, Lebron James stood up for the guy and even Ed Shultz of MSNBC defended Sherman saying that him being criticized was unfair.

And goodness knows how many of the young kids of today look up to Lebron James, Richard Sherman, and other standout players and how much length they go to, to emulate, or be like, their favorites.

It's also no wonder Nike, Reebok, Gatorade and other major sponsors spend as much as they do endorsing these athletes, regardless of how 'thuggish' they seem to appear at times.

We all know that in our society, money talks!

As such, there is ample proof that there exists in our society a 'thug mentality' or 'thug culture,' and mostly in the ranks of younger black males.

And if you look closely at Trayvon Martin and Michael Brown and the facts surrounding their deaths, and compare it to my analysis in this chapter, you might just agree it's highly possible that the word 'thug' played a bigger role in each of the young men's deaths than the media and the politically-correct mindset of reverse discrimination would allow you to believe.

I ask you to be sure and read the last chapter of this book, if you don't read a single other chapter.

In there I talk about how this 'Thug Mentality' or 'Thug Culture' is a barrier along with my politically-correct mindset of reverse discrimination and the pandering of blacks, to ever ending racism and achieving true equality of the races.

Chapter 26: How the "Thug Mentality"

and the Pandering of Blacks as a result of the Politically-Correct
Mindset of Reverse Discrimination is a
Barrier to Ending Racism

In ending this book, I imagine many of you would judge me a racist.

Sincerely, I am not. I truly believe in equality for all the races, and this book has been my attempt to get us back on the road toward that equality.

But there never will be equality of the races as long as society allows for the pandering of blacks the way that it does because of the politically-correct mindset of reverse discrimination that exists in society, the existence of which I hope this book has proven, or as least shed some light upon.

And as long as society, and the media, keep allowing and encouraging endless accusations by blacks, of discrimination here, and discrimination there, I am afraid the ugly monster of racism will continue to terrify the society in which we live.

I wonder if Al Sharpton, Jesse Jackson and the blacks of today realize that crying 'wolf,' or discrimination of whites against blacks every other day, and for every little situation where a black has possibly been wronged, does not set well with most whites, or what I have referred to herein several times as the silent white majority?

And especially in situations where the true facts, (not necessarily those presented by the media) show there was clearly NO discrimination?

When that happens to be the case, for your information, most whites everywhere, and yes, me included, don't even want to listen to it.

In cases like Trayvon Martin's where a jury clearly heard all the evidence and said race was not involved, yet the media created a circus, and could only do so by calling George Zimmerman a "white Hispanic" in order to make the case about race at all.

In cases like Ferguson, where Michael Brown had proven himself a felonious "thug" by assaulting a store owner and then assaulting the police office by attempting to grab his gun.

In cases like the Jena Six, where 'hate crimes' were not even considered for blacks assaulting a white student, sending him to the hospital, and those assaults were clearly motivated by, and only happened because of, race. Yet a 'hate crime' was filed for the hanging of a noose from the back of a pickup.

Now in these three cases, not only was there clearly NO DISCRIMINATION, but the end results, or the outcomes, proved beyond a shadow of a doubt that there does exist in our society a politically-correct mindset of reverse discrimination, and that blacks are pandered to in our society.

In Trayvon Martin's case, it was the extensive media coverage, slanted with a storyline that discrimination against blacks had occurred, a federal investigation, statements from the President, protests and marches screaming "Justice for Trayvon." Yet we never heard the same for the many cases I cited where whites had been killed by blacks.

In Ferguson, it was again the extensive media coverage about discrimination, where, "an unarmed black teenager was killed by a white cop," constant protests and even violence which was downplayed in the media, another federal investigation, but again, no mention of simultaneous cases where whites had been killed by blacks. Nor were the races of the parties involved even mentioned for a case shortly later where a black muslim man shot two non-black cops in Brooklyn.

Or back to Jena where not only were the blacks who assaulted the white student, NOT prosecuted for 'hate crimes,' their sentences were even reduced or the charges amended way down to almost nothing, because of presumed discrimination by a white Southern judicial system. But four months in jail for a noose?

The silent white majority I speak of, I am guessing, is sick and tired of discrimination against blacks being thrown in our faces in cases such as these, as we hear and see the cries of racism so one-sidedly played out on our televisions, newspapers and the internet.

And on top of that, we are constantly bombarded with all the other double standards in society as to race, as blacks are pandered to over and over again, which further support and help prove the existence of my politically-correct mindset of reverse discrimination.

A Congressional Black Caucus but not a White Congressional Caucus.

A Black Coaches Association but not a White Coaches Association.

African American Museums, partially funded by the federal government but no White American Museums.

Black Image Awards for black movies but no White Image Awards for white movies.

Historically Black Colleges and Universities, partially funded by the government, but no Historically White Colleges and Universities.

Black History Month for the celebration of African American culture but no White History Month to celebrate White American culture. Not even one white pride billboard in Harrison, Arkansas.

Black Entertainment Television but no White Entertainment Television.

Affirmative Action, or actual legislative or executively ordered reverse discrimination. Reverse discrimination is the law!

Confederate Flags are taboo, (even hoop skirts!) but Black Power salutes? No problem.

'Hate Crimes' being heavily considered and used against whites, but rarely considered and even more rarely used against blacks.

A huge outcry and presumption about the racial profiling of blacks, with never a consideration that perhaps blacks are just committing more crimes.

Demands for more black coaches for collegiate and professional football and basketball teams, when the football fields of the NFL and NCAA and the basketball courts of the NBA and NCAA are routinely filled with 80 to 90 percent black players.

Blacks can use the word "nigger" or "nigga" at will, referring to each other, or in rap songs, but dare a white mention the word and a career is ruined, apologies demanded.

A television show can be so blatantly entitled, "Blackish" but no show exists entitled, "Whiteish."

And then let us make sure not to forget some of the absolutely absurd claims of discrimination by blacks?

A cry of racism for a rodeo clown wearing an Obama mask. Yet comedians have trashed white presidents for decades without such a cry.

A ridiculous allegation made by Al Sharpton, again crying 'wolf,' that the Oscars are too white.

And then added to all this is the "Thug Mentality" or "Thug Culture," which I feel pervades the black, and particularly the younger black, community.

Total disrespect for authority, law enforcement, women and children.

Words in songs that straighten the hair on white people, and some blacks, everywhere. "Nigga" this, "nigga" that. The F word, constantly. "mother f en" this, "f" that.

Words that talk about "popping" cops and slapping down "bitches" and "hoes."

Pants hanging half way down their asses, underwear showing, tank tops, tattoos all over, excessive jewelry and bling, exaggerated corn rows or dreads for hair.

I wonder if the black community even realizes that these 'thugs' of today may be the only blacks that many white Americans, through television and other media ever see, or ever 'choose' to see? I dare say that most whites are very comfortable simply assuming that all blacks are that way.

And even though CNN spent most of the next week attempting to downplay his words, many whites, including myself, will always picture Michael Brown's step father Louis Head, as he jumped up on the platform alongside Michael Brown's mother, right after the grand jury's non-indictment of officer Darren Wilson, in t-shirt, pants hanging down off his ass, underwear showing, as he so angrily and vehemently screamed, "Burn this bitch down" over and over and over again.

Do you think for one minute that the silent white majority, and even some blacks for that matter, want to listen to people that look, speak and act like that?

And that can be a rhetorical question.

I feel this "Thug Mentality" or "Thug Culture" is clearly a barrier to whites ever giving blacks the time of day. And especially when it exists alongside all of the aforementioned double standards of reverse discrimination, and the excessive pandering of blacks in every walk of life.

I think I am speaking for most whites when I say we are tired of Al Sharpton and Jesse Jackson.

We are tired of all the whining about racism, and especially in cases where it clearly doesn't exist.

We are tired of the black-happy media which perpetuates and amplifies racism in a world where so many of these other double standards exist, which prove that blacks are actually pandered to, and given preferential treatment over whites when it comes to race, and claims of discrimination.

Trust me, we don't want to hear it.

And lastly, I fear the more these things are crammed down the throats of white people everywhere, the more likely racism will continue to exist in our society.

That's right, racism will not end.

And we will continue to live in a world where movies can be titled, "White Men Can' Jump," but there will never be one titled, "Black Men Can't Read."

There's not a new civil rights movement.

Not even close.

Dr Martin Luther King, Jr. and his followers protested with class and looked and acted (non-violent) like respectable men and women as they fought for basic human dignity and basic human rights. And MLK did this with impeccable timing, picking just the right battles at just the right times.

The so-called new civil rights leaders of today aren't even worthy to shine his shoes as they cry out for the Oscars to be more black, or a clown to be investigated for wearing an Obama mask.

So is there a politically-correct mindset of reverse discrimination ingrained in our society?

Black Pandering

You tell me.

Or just let that question be rhetorical too.

There is one final point that I have previously not made in this book, saving it for here. This involves how the blacks of today choose to call and label themselves "African Americans."

Go see "Selma."

In the final scene of that movie after the marchers had endured their way from Selma to Montgomery, Dr. Martin Luther King, Jr. made a speech on the steps of the capital of Alabama.

In that speech he talked about, "The only normalcy.... is the normalcy that recognizes the dignity and worth of all of God's children.... the normalcy of brotherhood, the normalcy of true peace, the normalcy of justice."

I truly believe Dr. King was envisioning a day, and I'm sure he would have hoped it had happened by now, when all of us referred to ourselves and to each other, as simply--Americans.

Not African Americans, not White Americans, not Blacks, or Whites, not Caucasian Americans, or Asian Americans, or Hispanics, or even White Hispanics.

Just Americans. The way it should be.

And here is another, and final, takeaway from this book-- Racism will end when people stop talking about racism.

And equal just happens.

CPSIA information can be obtained at www.ICGtesting.com
Printed in the USA
LVOW07s0953250715

447541LV00001B/1/P